THE ECONOMIC
IMPACT OF THE 2014
EBOLA EPIDEMIC

THE ECONOMIC IMPACT OF THE 2014 EBOLA EPIDEMIC

Short- and Medium-Term Estimates for West Africa

 WORLD BANK GROUP

ISBN (paper): 978-1-4648-0438-0
ISBN (electronic): 978-1-4648-0422-9
DOI: 10.1596/978-1-4648-0438-0

Cover design: Bill Pragluski, Critical Stages.

Library of Congress Cataloging-in-Publication Data has been requested.

Contents

Tables

Foreword

The current Ebola epidemic, which began in Guinea in late 2013 and then spread to Liberia and Sierra Leone over the first six months of 2014, is by far the largest in history. With more than 5,000 suspected deaths at the time of writing, this outbreak is more than 17 times as lethal as the next most serious Ebola outbreak, which took place 38 years ago in the Democratic Republic of Congo. Furthermore, health specialists believe that both cases and deaths are dramatically underreported; exactly by how much is unknown. With a fatality rate exceeding 50 percent, the primary tragedy of this epidemic is the thousands of lives lost.

Unfortunately, mortality is but one of the scars that Ebola will leave in its wake. As with all diseases, this Ebola outbreak has a significant direct economic impact: Households are losing breadwinners and have fewer resources to invest in enterprise and savings. Individuals are losing productive time as they care for sick relatives and friends. However, this Ebola epidemic is different from other disease outbreaks. The main economic impact comes not from the deaths, the sickness, and the time caring for the ill, as tragic as those are. Instead, fear is driving the majority of economic impacts associated with Ebola. Other illnesses, like malaria or childhood diarrhea or even HIV, have relatively well-known forms of both prevention and treatment. This is not the case for Ebola, where treatments have limited success and many people have a limited understanding of how it is spread. As a result, some individuals who have not contracted the disease are taking extreme actions, called "aversion behavior," to avoid exposure. Flights are cancelled, mining operations are slowed or stopped, and trade slows to a trickle.

It may seem mundane to speak of an economic impact in the face of a medical tragedy. But this economic impact has a human face. Guinea, Liberia, and Sierra Leone are all net food importers, which means that slowing food trade with their neighbors translates into food shortages. Cash crops that Guinean farmers hoped to sell face few buyers; and laid-off miners in Sierra Leone and Liberia are unable to feed their families. Schools have been closed: When they open again, some of the former students will not return because their families cannot pay the accompanying costs or because the children have been forced to start working. Mothers who would normally seek pre-natal care and early childhood vaccinations will not do so for fear of catching Ebola at a health center. These interruptions in human capital investments have long-term consequences. The economic impact of Ebola means children missing meals and school lessons, and parents missing economic opportunities.

This report draws on the array of skills within the World Bank Group to examine the likely economic impacts of the Ebola epidemic through the end of 2015. It begins from a country perspective, using the best available data on economic activity to update forecasts for growth in Guinea, Liberia, and Sierra Leone over the next year. It then uses macroeconomic models of the global economy to predict, under two scenarios of potential spread of the epidemic, the likely impact for West Africa as a whole. The results are stark. Guinea, Liberia, and Sierra Leone have already been dramatically affected. If the epidemic is not contained swiftly, the economic impacts for those three countries as well as for West Africa as a whole could be catastrophic.

This work highlights the need to contain the epidemic through swift action by international partners and local governments alike. But it also underlines the need to provide support to mitigate the economic impacts—through fiscal support so that governments can continue providing essential services even while many of their own resources are focused on the health crisis and, over time, through renewed commercial investment. All three of the most affected countries, as well as the region as a whole, enjoyed healthy economic growth in advance of the crisis. The swift and coordinated actions of the international community may help limit the impact of this Ebola crisis to an interruption in that trajectory of sustained economic growth rather than a lengthy detour.

Makhtar Diop
Vice President for Africa
World Bank

Acknowledgments

This report was prepared at the request and under the leadership of Jim Yong Kim, President of the World Bank Group. It benefited from guidance from Makhtar Diop, World Bank Vice President for the Africa Region, and Marcelo Giugale, World Bank Senior Director of the Global Practice for Poverty Reduction and Economic Management.

The report was written jointly by a team drawn from the World Bank's Global Practice for Macroeconomics and Fiscal Management, the Office of the Chief Economist for the Africa Region, and the Development Prospects Group in the Development Economics Vice Presidency. It includes inputs provided by Timothy Bulman, César Calderón, Marcio Cruz, Sébastien Dessus, Yusuf Bob Foday, Delfin Go, Errol Graham, Hans Lofgren, Maryla Maliszewska, Anna Popova, Cyrus Talati, Hardwick Tchale, Mark Thomas, Ali Zafar, and Mead Over (from the Center for Global Development). The work was coordinated by David Evans under the overall guidance of Francisco Ferreira, Chief Economist for the Africa Region, and John Panzer, Director in the Global Practice for Poverty Reduction and Economic Management.

Reviewers provided helpful feedback on the report, including Shanta Devarajan, Soji Adeyi, James Thurlow (from the International Food Policy Research Institute), Eric Le Borgne, R. Sudharshan Canagarajah, Olga Jonas, Santiago Herrera, and Paola Agostini. The team also received helpful input from Alessandro Vespignani (from Northeastern University) regarding the likely spread of the epidemic.

The team accepts full responsibility for any errors.

Abbreviations

CDC	Centers for Disease Control and Prevention
CES	constant elasticity of substitution
CGE	computable general equilibrium
CIF	cost, insurance, and freight
EVD	Ebola virus disease
FAO	Food and Agriculture Organization
FDI	foreign direct investment
FOB	free-on-board
GDP	gross domestic product
GNF	Guinean franc
GTAP	Global Trade Analysis Project
MAMS	Maquette for Millennium Development Goal Simulations
MSF	Médecins Sans Frontières
SARS	severe acute respiratory syndrome
WFP	World Food Program
WHO	World Health Organization

Executive Summary

- Beyond the terrible toll in human lives and suffering, the Ebola epidemic currently afflicting West Africa is already having a measurable economic impact in terms of forgone output; higher fiscal deficits; rising prices; lower real household incomes and greater poverty. These economic impacts—estimated in this report using data from early October of 2014—include the costs of health care and forgone productivity of those directly affected, but more important, they arise from the aversion behavior of others in response to the disease.

- The short-term (2014) impact on output, estimated using on-the-ground data to inform revisions to sector-specific growth projections, is in the order of 2.1 percentage points (pp) of gross domestic product (GDP) in Guinea (reducing growth from 4.5 percent to 2.4 percent); 3.4 pp of GDP in Liberia (reducing growth from 5.9 percent to 2.5 percent) and 3.3 pp of GDP in Sierra Leone (reducing growth from 11.3 percent to 8.0 percent). This forgone output for these three countries corresponds to US$359 million in 2013 prices.

- The short-term fiscal impacts are also large, at US$113 million (5.1 percent of GDP) for Liberia; US$95 million (2.1 percent of GDP for Sierra Leone) and US$120 million (1.8 percent of GDP) for Guinea. These estimates are best viewed as lower-bounds. Slow containment scenarios would almost certainly lead to even greater impacts and corresponding financing gaps in both 2014 and 2015. Governments are mitigating some of these impacts on their budgets through reallocation of resources, but much international support is still needed.

- As it is far from certain that the epidemic will be fully contained by December 2014 and in light of the considerable uncertainty about its future trajectory, two alternative scenarios are used to estimate the medium-term (2015) impact of the epidemic, extending to the end of calendar year 2015. A "Low Ebola" scenario corresponds to rapid containment within the three most severely affected countries (henceforth the "core three countries"), while "High Ebola" corresponds to slower containment in the core three countries, with some broader regional contagion.

- The medium-term impact (2015) on output in Guinea is estimated to be negligible under Low Ebola, and 2.3 pp of GDP under High Ebola. In Liberia, it is estimated to be 5.8 pp of GDP under Low Ebola, or 12.0 pp of GDP under High Ebola. In Sierra Leone, the impact would be 1.2 pp of GDP under Low Ebola, and 8.9 pp under High Ebola. The estimates of the GDP lost as a result of the epidemic in the core three countries (for calendar year 2015 alone) sum to US$129 million under Low Ebola (implying some recovery from 2014), and US$815 million under High Ebola (in 2013 dollars).

- Over the medium term, however, both epidemiological and economic contagion in the broader sub-region of West Africa is likely. To account for the probable spillovers on neighboring countries, we use the Bank's integrated, multi-country general equilibrium model (LINKAGE), to estimate the medium-term impact on output for West Africa as a whole. Under Low Ebola, the loss in GDP for the sub-region is estimated to be US$2.2 billion in 2014 and US$1.6 billion in 2015. Under High Ebola, the estimates are US$7.4 billion in 2014 and US$25.2 billion in 2015. These estimates of forgone output are presented in table ES.1, alongside those for the core three countries, reported above. Additional analysis for Liberia indicates that the percent losses are even more severe for household consumption, resulting in drastic increases in poverty rates. The reasons for this, which are also at work in the other countries,

TABLE ES.1
Lost GDP Due to Ebola, in Dollars and as a Percentage of 2013 GDP

	Short-term impact (2014)	Medium-term impact (2015—Low Ebola)	Medium-term impact (2015—High Ebola)
Guinea (million)	130 (2.1 pp)	−43 (0.7 pp)	142 (2.3 pp)
Liberia (million)	66 (3.4 pp)	113 (5.8 pp)	234 (12.0 pp)
Sierra Leone (million)	163 (3.3 pp)	59 (1.2 pp)	439 (8.9 pp)
Core three countries (million)	359	129	815
West Africa (billion)	2.2–7.4	1.6	25.2

Source: World Bank and International Monetary Fund (IMF) estimates.
Note: All values are expressed in 2013 US dollars. pp = percentage points.

relate to Ebola-induced barriers to domestic and foreign trade, which divert labor to service sectors and lead to disproportionate increases in consumer prices.

- The take-away messages from this analysis are that the economic impacts are already very serious in the core three countries—particularly Liberia and Sierra Leone—and could become catastrophic under a slow-containment, High Ebola scenario. In broader regional terms, the economic impacts could be limited if immediate national and international responses succeed in containing the epidemic and mitigating aversion behavior. The successful containment of the epidemic in Nigeria and Senegal so far is evidence that this is possible, given some existing health system capacity and a resolute policy response.

- If, on the other hand, the epidemic spreads into neighboring countries, some of which have much larger economies, the cumulative two-year impact could reach US$32.6 billion by the end of 2015—almost 2.5 times the combined 2013 GDP of the core three countries.

- A swift policy reaction by the international community is crucial. With the potential economic costs of the Ebola epidemic being so high, very substantial containment and mitigation expenditures would be cost-effective if they successfully avert the worst epidemiological outcomes. To mitigate the medium-term economic impact of the outbreak, current efforts by many partners to strengthen the health systems and fill the fiscal gaps in the core three countries are key priorities. These efforts should also be supplemented by investments in those countries and in their neighbors to renew the confidence of international tourism, travel, trade, and investment partners.

- Finally, there are two important caveats. First, this analysis does not take into account the longer-term impacts generated by mortality, failure to treat other health conditions due to aversion behavior and lack of supply capacity, school closings and dropouts, and other shocks to livelihoods. It is truly focused on the short- and medium-term inputs over the next 18 months.

- Second, these estimates are subject to considerable uncertainty, arising not only from the usual and well-known problems associated with economic forecasting and data scarcity, but also from the unusually high degree of uncertainty associated with the future epidemiological path of Ebola and with people's behavioral responses to it. All the analysis in this report therefore represents best-effort estimates under documented assumptions and modeling choices, but the margins of error associated with them are inevitably large. The scenarios should be read and interpreted accordingly.

Introduction

Overview

The 2014 outbreak of the Ebola Virus Disease[1] in West Africa[2] has taken a devastating human toll. Although the outbreak originated in rural Guinea, it has hit hardest in Liberia and Sierra Leone, in part because it has reached urban areas in these two countries—a factor that distinguishes this outbreak from previous episodes elsewhere. As of early November 2014, there had been more than 5,000 recorded deaths out of more than 14,000 probable, suspected, or confirmed cases of Ebola (WHO 2014a). Experts fear that the true numbers may be two to four times larger due to underreporting (WHO 2014b).[3] Misery and suffering have been intense, especially in Liberia where doctors have had to turn patients away for lack of space in Ebola treatment centers.

Inevitably, before the outbreak is contained the human impacts will increase considerably beyond these numbers. Epidemiological estimates are acknowledged as highly uncertain and are not the subject of this report. What is certain is that limiting the human cost will require significant financial resources, a rapid response, and a concerted partnership between international partners and the affected countries. Particularly in Liberia and Sierra Leone, government capacity is already overrun and the epidemic is impacting economic activity and budgetary resources.

This report informs the response to the Ebola epidemic by presenting best-effort estimates of its macroeconomic and fiscal effects. These impacts are constantly changing; this report uses economic data from early October 2014 to estimate the potential economic and fiscal impacts. Any such exercise is necessarily highly imprecise due to limited data and many uncertain factors, but it is still necessary in order to plan the economic assistance that must accompany the immediate humanitarian response.

The goal is to help affected countries to recover and return to the robust economic growth they had experienced until the onset of this crisis.

Channels of Impact

The impact of the Ebola epidemic on economic well-being operates through two distinct channels. First are the direct and indirect effects of the sickness and mortality themselves, which consume health-care resources and subtract people either temporarily or permanently from the labor force. Second are the behavioral effects resulting from the fear of contagion, which in turn leads to a fear of association with others and reduces labor force participation, closes places of employment, disrupts transportation, motivates some governments to close land borders and restrict entry of citizens from afflicted countries, and motivates private decision makers to disrupt trade, travel, and commerce by canceling scheduled commercial flights and reducing shipping and cargo services. In the recent history of infectious disease outbreaks such as the SARS (severe acute respiratory syndrome) epidemic of 2002–04 and the H1N1 (swine flu) epidemic of 2009, behavioral effects are believed to have been responsible for as much as 80 or 90 percent of the total economic impact of the epidemics (Lee and McKibbin 2003).

The first of these channels, consisting of the labor force and health expenditure impacts arising from the direct and indirect effects of the epidemic, closely tracks the number of suspected and actual cases of the disease (see figure 1.1). The second, or behavioral channel, is less sensitive to the actual number of cases of Ebola because it is driven by aversion behavior, and it is potentially more sensitive to information and public response. For example, employers who learn how to protect themselves and their workers from contagion will reopen workplaces and resume production and investment. Similarly, governments that demonstrate they have controlled the epidemic and have resumed normal activity will inspire confidence in both domestic and international economic agents to resume their former pace of economic exchange.

Structure of the Report

This document presents the World Bank's preliminary estimates of the economic impact of the Ebola outbreak in West Africa for 2014 and 2015. Section 2 presents a single set of 2014 estimates for Liberia, Sierra Leone, and Guinea, based on available data on current economic activity as well

FIGURE 1.1
Broad Channels of Short-Term Economic Impact

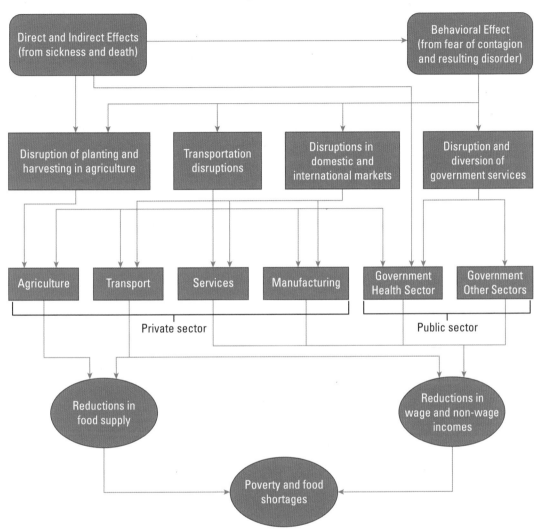

as assumptions about the short-term impact. It also presents data on the limited current impacts on other countries in the region. Section 3 presents estimates for the impact by the end of 2015 for Liberia, Sierra Leone, and Guinea, as well as estimates for West Africa as a whole. Because the epidemic and the behavioral responses to it have more time to diverge over the course of 2015, Section 3 presents two scenarios for 2015, which vary in the optimism of their assumptions regarding the epidemic and the success of donor and government policy and efforts to control it.

SECTION 2

Short-Term Effects and Fiscal Impacts

Introduction

The economic impact of the Ebola crisis is being felt acutely right now by the three directly affected countries. Limited impacts are even being felt among some neighboring countries. Both the limited available survey data and anecdotal evidence suggest impacts on agriculture, mining, services, and other sectors. Estimates of the impact of the crisis for this year—2014—for the three countries are built up from sector components, based on the impact seen so far on economic activity. Representatives of economic sectors were contacted to assess changes to economic activity from the evidence gathered. For example, mining officials provided metrics of the extent to which Ebola was affecting current activity and plans for future investment. The projections also rely on leading indicators considered to be good predictors of economic activity. Cement imports and sales, for example, are used to estimate the impact on construction activity and thereby on services. Data on agricultural exports as well as information regarding the stage(s) of the crop cycle interrupted by the crisis were used to estimate production shocks. Hotel occupancy rates, airline traffic, and airport activity provide metrics for the transport and tourism sub-sectors, as do the closure of borders and reductions in recorded cross-border trade.

In all cases, estimates of the impact of Ebola are compared with previous projections by the World Bank and the International Monetary Fund in the absence of Ebola. Other price information is also incorporated: nominal exchange rates, parallel exchange rates (if any), fuel prices,

9

and prices of a few other key goods, all serve as indicators of supply bot-
tlenecks and changes in investor or consumer behavior.

Fiscal impact has been estimated on the basis of actual year-to-date
revenues, projected shortfalls, and additional expenditures related to the
crisis. Revenue shortfalls are determined by disaggregating government
revenues and focusing on areas most likely to be affected by the crisis,
such as import taxes and taxes on expatriate personnel. Expenditure estimates are based on spending plans of the Ministries of Finance in each
country, as a part of the overall Ebola containment effort. These plans
include purchases of goods and supplies, core logistics, salaries and hazard
pay for emergency workers, training, and investment in rural health
centers.

Short-run estimates of the economic impact assume no further disruptions in international supply chains, such as the cutting-off of countries from international shipping, which would exacerbate the above
effects. Although it is true that there have been some border closings,
these borders tend to be quite porous. More severe scenarios are only
considered from 2015 onward in the region-wide impact scenarios. The
estimates in this section presume a resumption of normal economic activities within six to nine months. The economic estimates that follow are
not derived as explicit functions of infection or mortality rates but reflect
both observed and speculated individual, corporate, and government
behavioral responses to the epidemic.

Despite graphic illustrations of disruption in sub-sectors or regions
suggested by the indicators, the overall effects on projected economic
activity in terms of GDP growth in 2014 are not as sharp as one might
have expected.[4] In large measure, this reflects the fact that (in Liberia
and Sierra Leone) the emergence and spread of Ebola did not begin to
have a profound effect until the second half of 2014. Thus, despite sharp
reductions in growth in many sectors and sub-sectors, the overall result
for the year is moderated by robust growth during the first half of the
year. In contrast, the story for Guinea is somewhat different: The
economic effect of Ebola has been relatively less pronounced because
the health response to the initial outbreaks was quite effective. In any
event, the examples used in the country-specific analyses below are
intended to provide a snapshot of the dynamic situation on the ground
in each of these countries.

The information and data available for each of the three countries
vary. Accordingly, the degree of disaggregation of the country-level estimates varies, as do the confidence levels attached to some elements due
to imperfect information. Nonetheless, the estimates are built up from
the production side of the national accounts, comprising agriculture,

forestry, and fisheries, industry (including mining and manufacturing), and services.

The fiscal tables combine revenue losses and higher spending requirements—mainly in health, security, and social protection—to estimate a change in the fiscal gap. While the latter are based on explicit new expenditure requirements identified as a result of the Ebola emergency and are financed through the countries' budgets, it is not generally possible to disentangle all the revenue losses in the same manner. In such cases, the text acknowledges revenue underperformance and identifies its magnitude.

Liberia

Liberia is one of the poorest countries in Africa with a population of 4 million, per capita income of US$410, and almost 60 percent of the population below the national poverty line. More than half of the population is urban, including those living in densely populated areas around the capital city of Monrovia. About three-quarters of the labor force is engaged in informal activities, mainly agriculture, itinerant mining, and commerce. Despite its post-conflict fragility and poor social conditions, Liberia had been growing steadily prior to the Ebola outbreak under a regime of stable economic management, aided by efforts to improve public sector governance, and an expansion of extractive industries.

Liberia is currently the country most severely affected by the Ebola crisis. Since the first case of the Ebola virus was reported in March 2014, the virus has spread quickly, particularly since July, to cover most of the country. Nonetheless, current decreases in the rates of infection and death suggest that the crisis has reached an inflection point.

Impact on economic activities

Since the escalation of the Ebola outbreak in July 2014, there has been a sharp disruption of economic activity across sectors. The largest economic effects of the crisis are not the direct costs (mortality, morbidity, caregiving, and the associated losses in working days), but rather those resulting from changes in behavior—driven by fear—which have resulted in generally lower levels of employment, income, and demand for goods and services.

Despite early signs that the initial fear-based behavioral response is abating among Liberians, as evidenced by increased activity in local

TABLE 2.1
Liberia—Estimated GDP Impact of Ebola (2014)

	Sector contribution to growth shock (%)	Pre-Ebola growth projection (June 2014)	Revised growth projection
Real growth in GDP	—	*5.9*	*2.5*
Agriculture	18.0	3.5	1.3
Forestry	–0.1	2.0	2.0
Mining	27.3	4.4	–1.3
Manufacturing	4.6	9.6	5.0
Services	50.2	8.1	4.0

Source: World Bank and IMF estimates.

markets (about 80 percent of small and medium enterprises remain open), the initial estimate of a 3.5 percentage point reduction in GDP growth for 2014 (from 5.9 percent to 2.5 percent) remains optimistic. Table 2.1 shows revised estimates of GDP growth in 2014, with the contribution of each sector. A deepening of the crisis over the remaining months could diminish overall GDP growth still further.

Mining

The mining sector accounts for about 17 percent of GDP and 56 percent of the US$559 million worth of total exports in 2013. Production and exports are dominated by two large iron ore mining companies, ArcelorMittal and China Union. Production at the largest mining company (ArcelorMittal) is holding steady with production of approximately 3.3 million tons up to August—on track to achieve planned production of 5.2 million tons by the end of 2014. However, investments to expand capacity to 15 million tons per year have been put on hold. The second major mining company, China Union, which had projected production of approximately 2.4 million tons for 2014, closed its operation temporarily in August, perhaps because its mining operation was closer to the epicenter of the outbreak. Furthermore, restrictions on the movement of people have severely curtailed artisanal mining, including of gold and diamonds. Overall, the mining sector is expected to show a small contraction of 1.3 percent in 2013 compared with an initial projection for growth above 4 percent.

Agriculture

The agricultural sector accounts for about one-quarter of Liberia's GDP, but nearly half of the total employed workforce and three-quarters of the rural workforce is engaged in the sector. Both export and domestic agriculture have been severely affected by the crisis. Production and shipments of rubber—the single most important agricultural export for Liberia—have been disrupted by the reduced mobility of the workforce and by difficulty in getting the products to the ports due to the implementation of quarantine zones. Rubber exports, which were initially expected to be about US$148 million in 2014, could be as much as 20 percent lower.

Large investments in palm oil planting, including by the world's largest producer of palm oil, Sime Darby, have slowed due to the evacuation of managerial and supervisory personnel, and the focus has shifted to maintenance. Sime Darby's planned construction of a US$10 million modern oil palm mill, for which construction started in July 2014 and completion was expected in 2015, is also now on hold.

In domestic agriculture, the main food growing areas—in Lofa County in the northwest part of the country—are also those most affected by the outbreak of Ebola and have been quarantined. Farms have been abandoned. Even in cases where farming operations are ongoing, the shortage of labor as a result of the quarantine and the migration of some families from these areas at the onset of the outbreak has affected both the harvesting and replanting of several crops, including rice, Liberia's key staple. In addition, quarantine zones and the restrictions on movement of persons have adversely affected food transport and marketing, resulting in food shortages and price increases.

Manufacturing

Liberia's manufacturing sector, which accounts for only about 4 percent of GDP and is already hard-pressed by weak infrastructure, has been adversely affected by reduced demand as a result of the crisis. Liberia's small manufacturing sector is dominated by the cement and beverage sub-sectors, which together account for nearly 90 percent of manufacturing output. The production of paints, candles, bottled water, and mattresses comprises the remaining output. The adverse shock to the construction sector as a result of the quarantines has resulted in substantially lower demand for cement (figure 2.1). Cement sales fell by nearly 60 percent between July and September, well beyond seasonal effects related to the onset of the rainy season. There has also been reduced

FIGURE 2.1
Liberia—Cement Sales (2010–14)

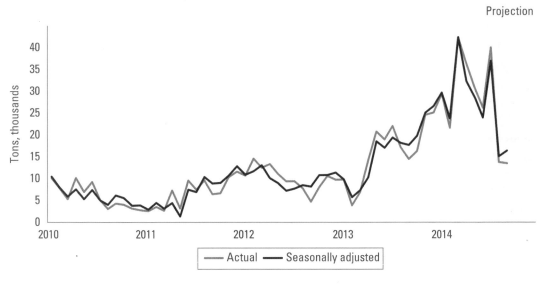

Source: World Bank calculations based on data from the Liberia Cement Corporation.

demand for beverages from the hotel and restaurant sub-sector, as the disruption to commercial flights has resulted in fewer business and tourist arrivals. The Ebola crisis has exacerbated the situation for an already weak beverage sub-sector, which had seen a 30 percent fall in beer production in the first quarter of 2014.

Services

The service sector, which comprises approximately half of the Liberian economy and employs nearly 45 percent of the labor force, has been hardest hit by the Ebola crisis. Wholesale and retail traders have reported a 50–75 percent drop in turnover relative to the normal amount for the trading period. The reduction has been largest in markets serving expatriates. Both commercial and residential construction activities, which were booming before the crisis, appear to be on hold, as reflected by the sharp fall in cement sales since June 2014 (figure 2.1).[5] Government construction activities in the energy and transport sectors have also come to a halt as contractors have declared *force majeure* and evacuated key personnel.

The domestic transport sub-sector has also been severely affected by the crisis. One indicator of this has been the sharp drop in fuel sales, with petrol and diesel sales down by 21 and 35 percent (figure 2.2). Emergency regulations limiting taxis to 4 passengers have raised the cost of domestic travel.

FIGURE 2.2
Liberia—Fuel Sales (2010–14)

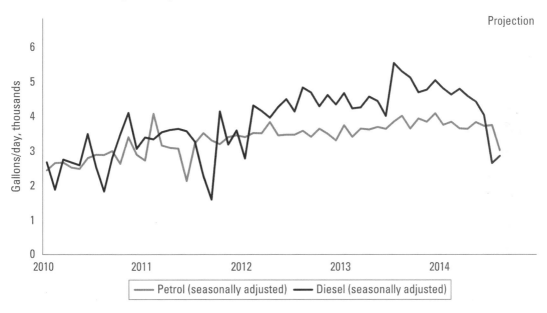

Source: World Bank calculations based on data from Liberia Petroleum Refining Company.

The cost of transporting goods has also seen increases, in some cases by 50 percent, partly reflecting the more difficult road conditions during the rainy season (May–October), as well as the disruptions arising from having to negotiate the area quarantines imposed to control the spread of Ebola.

The hotel and restaurants sub-sector has been adversely affected by the reduction of commercial flights to Liberia, from 27 weekly flights until August to only 6 at the beginning of September. Average hotel occupancy has dropped from upwards of 70 percent before the crisis to about 30 percent now. Some hotels have reported occupancy as low as 10 percent as a result of the crisis. As a direct result, hotel workers have either been laid-off or had their working days reduced by half.

Food prices and inflation

The disruption to harvesting and transport, as well as border closings and area quarantines—including in one of the primary agricultural production areas—have led to rising prices, with domestic food prices experiencing particular acceleration since June. In addition, panic buying has increased the demand for food staples, pushing their prices up (figure 2.3). There are also concerns that increased shipping insurance for ships transporting goods to Liberia could further drive up the price of imported foods and fuel.

FIGURE 2.3
Liberia—Inflation and Food Prices (2014)

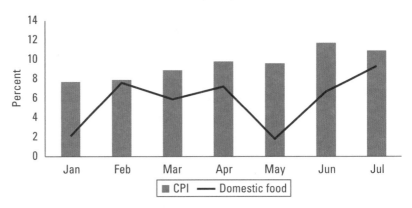

Source: World Bank calculations based on data from Liberia Institute of Statistics and Geo-Information Services. CPI = consumer price index.

External sector

The Ebola crisis has had a substantial impact on regional and international travel to Liberia, with direct effects on the hotel, transport, and restaurant sub-sectors in particular. In the short term, exports (mainly rubber and iron ore) have held, and the reductions in imports (including of capital goods owing to delayed investments) have resulted in an improvement in the balance of payments, as reflected in the modest appreciation of the exchange rate in July (figure 2.4). However, this position is unlikely to be sustained going forward with the expected increased demand for imported food, the fall-off in foreign direct investment (FDI), and adversely affected exports. For sea transport, the impact has been limited so far, largely due to pre-programmed scheduling contracts. However, there are indications that forward scheduling is weakening. Volumes of containers coming into Liberia are down 30 percent from normal levels in August.

Fiscal impact

The fiscal impact of the Ebola crisis in Liberia has already been substantial, estimated at over US$100 million (5.1 percent of GDP) for 2014 before budgetary reallocations, and the direct and contingent fiscal costs continue to rise (see table 2.2). On the revenue side, government data up to the first week of September showed total revenue collection of US$80.4 million, representing a shortfall of about US$10 million relative to pre-Ebola forecasts. Furthermore, the

FIGURE 2.4
Liberia—Movement of Daily Exchange Rate since the Crisis (2014)

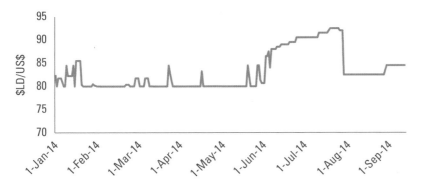

Source: Central Bank of Liberia.

TABLE 2.2
Liberia—Estimated Fiscal Impact of Ebola in 2014 (as estimated on October 1, 2014)
US$ millions

	Pre-Ebola projection (a)	Revised projection (b)	Net change (b)–(a)	
Tax and non-tax revenue	499.3	453.6	–45.7	
Current expenditure	441.9	509.1	67.2	
Health response	0	20	20	
Social response	0	47.2	47.2	
Current balance net of adjustments	57.4	–55.5	–112.9	Pre-response fiscal impact
Capital expenditure	275.6	255.6	–20	
Grants	59.6	59.6	0	
Overall balance	–158.6	–251.5	–92.9	Net fiscal impact
Overall balance (% of GDP)	–7.1	–11.8	–4.7	

Source: World Bank and IMF estimates.
Note: Liberia fiscal year 2015 covers July 1, 2014, through June 30, 2015.

government has so far revised its revenue target for September down from US$41.7 million to US$26.3 million—the lowest revenue collection since 2012. With the slowing of economic activity and weakness in tax administration (due to curfews and quarantines) total revenues for the year are likely to be about US$46 million below the initial forecast.

Of the total, current expenditure will increase by nearly US$70 million, while the government will reallocate US$20 million from capital to the current budget. The sharp reduction in fiscal revenues combined with the increased expenditure creates a *fiscal gap of about US$93 million to be financed*. This is likely to be a lower bound: These numbers were calculated in August and the impact of the crisis is increasing.

Sierra Leone

Sierra Leone has made good economic and social progress over the past 12 years, as indicated by steady progress in per capita income, which was US$680 in 2013. Despite the significant improvement, poverty is widespread, with 53 percent of the population living below the poverty line as of 2011. In rural areas, where the bulk of the population lives, the poverty rate is 66 percent. Three-quarters of the population is under 35 years of age, with the vast majority engaged in part-time activities related to agriculture, as there is little formal employment.

Ebola has now spread to all of the country's 13 districts, including the capital. The disease has taken a toll on the country's health system, with 5 doctors and more than 30 nurses among the dead. Most private hospitals have shut down, as have four public hospitals. The government imposed a nationwide curfew for three days, from September 19 to 21, and deployed some 28,500 persons across the country to visit every household.[6]

Impact on economic activities

The emergence of Ebola in rural Sierra Leone in May initially appeared to be an isolated event. By late July, however, the spread of Ebola led to the quarantining of the most severely affected districts and to restrictions on internal travel, market closures, and subsequently a number of other measures designed to reduce public gatherings. In late September, three more districts were quarantined. This has begun to have a marked effect on economic activity, one that is disproportionate to the human toll that Ebola has taken to date. The actions of economic agents are being driven by a high level of aversion behavior, and this may be considered the root

FIGURE 2.5
Sierra Leone—Weekly Cement Sales (2014)

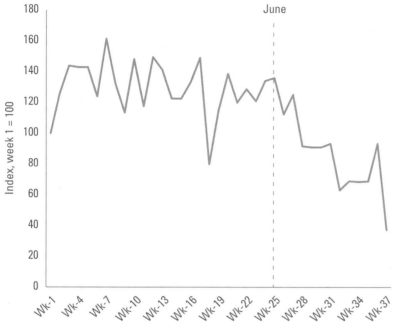

Source: World Bank calculations of cement factory sales.

cause of the unfolding slow down. Leading indicators of the slowdown in economic activity and aversion by the external community are captured by sharp reductions in cement sales and visitor arrivals (figures 2.5 and 2.6), although the drop in cement sales coincided with the onset of the wet season in May when cement sales would naturally decline due to reduced road-building. Likewise, a drop in diesel sales indicates reduced domestic trade (figure 2.7).

Despite the sharp slowdown now evident in many indicators, the effect of the severe disruption to economic activity in 2014 will be less than might be expected due to the broad-based and robust growth achieved over the first six months of the year. Overall projected economic growth is expected to slow to 8 percent in 2014 (table 2.3). A sharper decline may be expected in 2015.

Agriculture

Agriculture is the mainstay of the vast majority of the population and accounted for 50 percent of the economy in 2013. The two eastern districts—Kailahun and Kenema—where Ebola first emerged

FIGURE 2.6
Sierra Leone—Visitor Arrivals (2014)

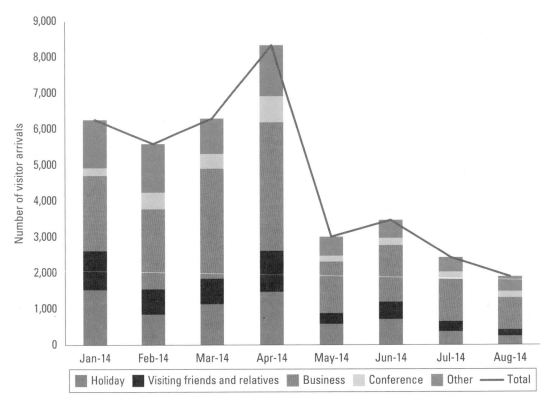

Source: Sierra Leone Immigration Department.

FIGURE 2.7
Sierra Leone—Diesel Fuel Sales Volume (2014)

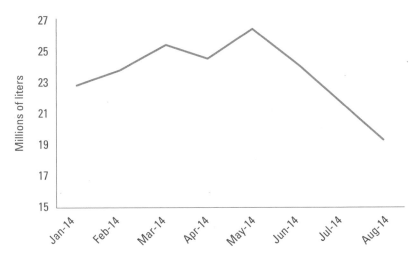

Source: Petroleum Directorate, Sierra Leone.

TABLE 2.3
Sierra Leone—Estimated GDP Impact of Ebola (2014)
Percent

	Contribution to growth shock	Initial projection (June 2014)	Revised projection
Real GDP growth	—	*11.3*	*8.0*
Agriculture	27.8	4.8	2.6
Industry of which mining	54.5 (39.6)	24.9 (27.3)	18.4 (21.8)
Services	17.7	7.7	5.7

Source: World Bank and IMF estimates.

are also the epicenter of the disease and home to one-fifth of the country's population. They contain the most productive agricultural areas in Sierra Leone, producing both the staple food—rice—and cash crops, such as cocoa and palm oil. According to data from the Ministry of Agriculture, Forestry and Food Security, the two districts together produce about 18 percent of the total domestic rice output. With expected production disruptions due to the quarantine-induced restrictions on farmer movements, it is very likely that national rice production for the 2014/15 season will be significantly affected. Furthermore, the closure of markets, internal travel restrictions, and the fear of infection has curtailed food trade and caused supply shortages. Although robust price data are not yet available, reports indicate rice price spikes of up to 30 percent in the Ebola-affected areas. These are further exacerbated by the country's heavy dependence on imported rice, with import volumes potentially down due to land border closures.

Reports indicate that farming activities are being disrupted with possible knock-on effects on the expected harvest for this season, particularly in the hardest hit areas. A Food and Agriculture Organization (FAO) rapid assessment in Kailahun indicated that at least 40 percent of farmers may have either abandoned their farms and moved to new, safer locations or died, leaving the farms unattended. (Some of these may have been short-term, initial reactions at the outset of the epidemic.) In certain key agro-ecological areas, about 90 percent of the plots are reported not to have been cultivated (FAO 2014). Current restrictions on movement are preventing cultivation from taking place. Moreover, farmers have expressed fear of meeting together or even sharing tools. As a result, they have missed some critical land husbandry activities in the recent planting season (which extends through July for rice), and it is likely that they will not have sufficient planting materials for the next planting season, as rice seeds have been consumed in light of recent food shortages.

Nationally, food accounts for 62 percent of household consumption expenditures, and 59 percent of rice growers are net buyers of rice, an indication that food insecurity is an important issue. This proportion increases sharply during the lean season—referred to locally as the hungry season—which is also the planting season, usually June to August. During this period, about 45 percent of the population, or 2.5 million people, do not have access to sufficient food. In the districts of Kenema, Kailahun, and Bo, an estimated 30 percent of the population is considered food insecure, a figure which will surely rise due to the spread of Ebola (figure 2.8).

The World Food Program (WFP) is leading the process of providing food to quarantined households, and their assessment indicates that over 1 million people are likely to be in dire need of food due to the direct and indirect impact of Ebola. The FAO and WFP have made calls for an emergency operation amounting to 65,000 tons of food to provide assistance to approximately 1.3 million of the most affected people in the three countries over a period of three months. Additional support in the provision of food rations to quarantined households has been provided by UNICEF and the World Bank.

The disruption to agriculture and food production will have particularly strong adverse effects on nutrition given the underlying rates of chronic malnutrition in the country. Chronic malnutrition is a serious problem in Sierra Leone, with 35 percent of children aged 6–59 months stunted and 10 percent severely stunted. Comparable stunting rates for

FIGURE 2.8
Sierra Leone—Share of Households with Insufficient Food Stocks (2011)

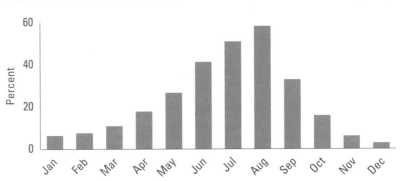

Source: World Food Program 2011.

Kenema and Kailahun were 41 and 42 percent, respectively, which is considered critical by the World Health Organization (WHO). School feeding programs provide nourishment to many children, but with the government-ordered closure of all educational institutions in the country until November, nearly 7,000 schools have been shut down, affecting close to 1.6 million children. The WFP has made a request to use school feeding program resources for the immediate emergency response to quarantined households.

Mining

Mining accounts for 85 percent of industry in Sierra Leone. (Industry, altogether, makes up nearly 20 percent of the economy.) Mining is dominated by the iron ore sector, which began production in late 2011 and already accounts for 16 percent of GDP. In addition, there are less significant operations in rutile, ilmenite, bauxite, and diamonds. To date, there has been little effect of Ebola on mining production, and the companies involved have indicated that they intend to maintain their originally planned production levels to the extent possible. Nonetheless, many are operating with reduced expatriate personnel and the risk of disruption remains. Moreover the two iron ore companies have been experiencing financial difficulties related to the prevailing low international price of iron ore. Notwithstanding that, the maintenance of planned iron ore production in 2014 will likely shield the overall economy from a sharper decline in growth due to Ebola. However, iron ore prices plummeted to 5-year lows in September 2014. This is likely to result in adverse effects on exports and government revenues through lower royalty receipts, which are based on the international iron ore prices.

Manufacturing

The manufacturing sector accounts for a mere 2 percent of the economy. Its importance is, however, disproportionate to its size, as it is an important employer in a country with very little in the way of paid employment opportunities. Most manufacturing enterprises are small scale and well-suited to the economic landscape, operating in the production of beer, soft drinks, paint, soap, cement, foam mattresses, and the like. Present indications suggest that the sector is faltering due to generally reduced demand in the economy. A case in point is the soft drinks sector, which has experienced a recent decline in sales attributed to Ebola (figure 2.9).

FIGURE 2.9
Sierra Leone—Soft Drink Sales (2014)

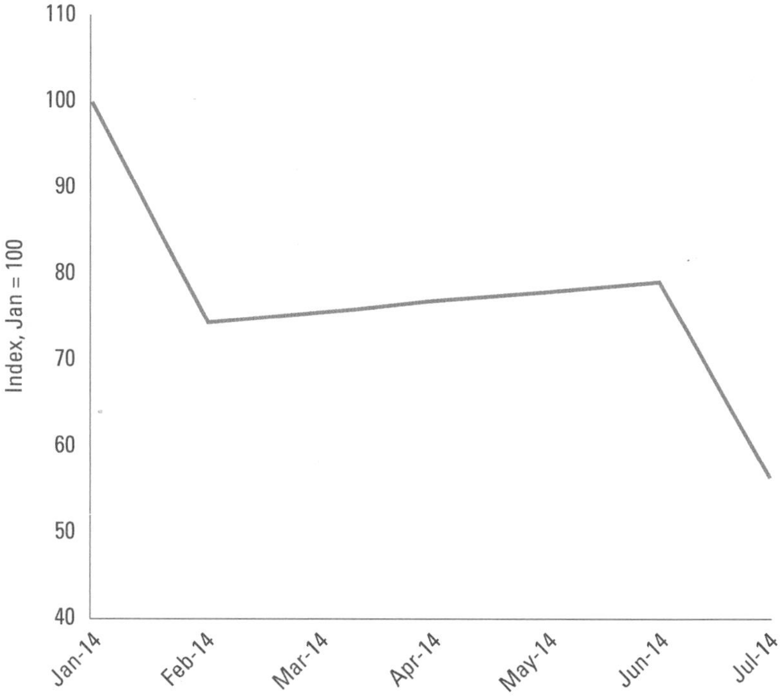

Source: Bank of Sierra Leone.

Construction

Like manufacturing, the construction industry is far more important to the economy than its 1 percent share would imply. This relates to its critical role in nearly all new investment and highlights its significance for future growth. Another key aspect of the sector is its labor intensity and the fact that it can utilize relatively unskilled labor, which is important in an economy with a large labor surplus, such as that of Sierra Leone. Thus, a booming construction sector is usually a good leading indicator of a flourishing economy. Exploiting cement sales as a good proxy for the state of the construction sector, it is evident that the construction sector has entered a downturn due to the advent of Ebola.

Services

The service sector accounts for 30 percent of the Sierra Leonean economy, and this vibrant sector provides both formal and informal employment to large numbers of people. The recent Ebola-induced closures and restrictions on markets, restaurants, bars, and nightclubs are having a severe dampening effect on the sector, as are the transportation restrictions. The nascent hospitality sector has been particularly hard hit by the cancellations of commercial flights to the country. The number of weekly flights serving Sierra Leone fell from 31 flights per week until August, to only 6 flights a week, as of September 1, increasing the country's isolation from international markets. The effects of this dramatic reduction in flight service on the hospitality sub-sector are illustrated by the findings of a recent survey of six hotels in Freetown, covering a total of 490 rooms. These establishments directly employed a little over 500 persons. Two of the hotels had closed down and laid off their employees because of the fall in occupancy. Most of the remainder had arranged for half the workforce to work for 15 days a month, on a rotating basis; others had shed workers. Occupancy rates plunged to 13 percent from usual year-round rates of 60–80 percent. The knock-on effects on others in the labor force linked to the hospitality sector is likely to be large. Commercial flight cancellations have both direct and indirect adverse effects: beyond reducing hotel occupancy, this has led to most airlines laying off staff and maintaining a skeleton crew of one or two employees. The water taxi and ferry sub-sectors are now idle, and many previously employed young men are inactive.

Another illustration of these linkages relates to the local brewery, which put planned investment on hold indefinitely and was considering closing its facility because of the fall in demand. Government estimates suggest that closure of the brewery would put up to 24,000 people out of work nationwide—mainly in the hospitality industry—and render another 2,000–2,500 households in agriculture without a breadwinner.

Food prices and inflation

The effect of the Ebola crisis on food prices remains ambiguous for the moment, though it appears certain that food prices will increase due to shortages caused by the crisis. Already there are reports of rice price increases of 30 percent in some markets in the afflicted areas. The consumer price index has recorded a slight uptick in food inflation in both June and July, attributed in part to the Ebola-related market closures and to the depreciation of the currency as well as to seasonal effects (figure 2.10).

External sector

The balance of payments financing gap will increase as imports—related to emergency health and food products—expand in the face of

FIGURE 2.10
Sierra Leone—Inflation and Food Prices (2014)

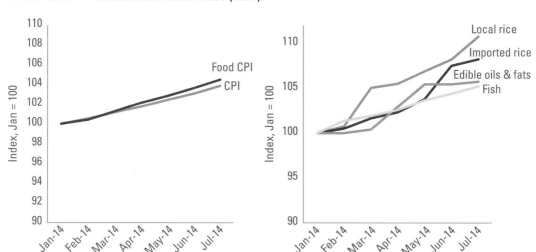

Source: Statistics Sierra Leone.

falling export earnings from minerals and agriculture. The Leone exchange rate has been relatively stable this year until June, when it began to depreciate against the U.S. dollar, altogether by about 6 percent (figure 2.11). The parallel market rate has seen a similar widening. This may relate to capital outflow in the face of current uncertainty and the aversion behavior it is causing. Remittances have remained steady (figure 2.12). International reserves have been stable during the year and were equivalent to about 2.5 months of imports at the end of August 2014.

The government is constantly revising its 2014 fiscal plan to take into account a rapidly changing and uncertain environment (table 2.4). Revenues are expected to fall in the second half of the year due to reduced economic activity and a probable reduction in tax compliance, all due to Ebola (about US$46 million). This compounds a preexisting challenge: The government also had to contend with revenue underperformance in the first half of the year, which totaled some US$11 million. Additionally, the recent historically low international price for iron ore will further reduce expected revenues in the second half of 2014. An emergency Ebola response plan will require increased recurrent spending (worth US$37 million), mostly for the health sector. Some of this is to be financed through a reallocation of capital spending, which still leaves an unfinanced gap of US$77 million. This figure is likely to be a lower bound as the situation remains volatile.

FIGURE 2.11
Sierra Leone—Exchange Rate (2014)

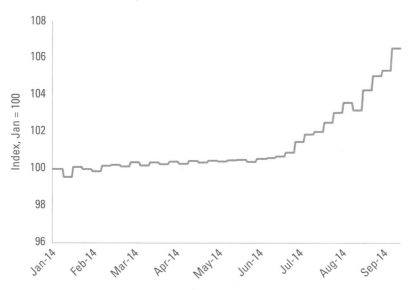

Source: Bank of Sierra Leone.

FIGURE 2.12
Sierra Leone—Remittances (2013–14)

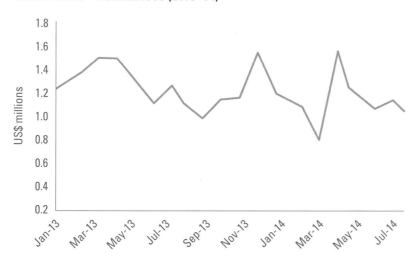

Source: Bank of Sierra Leone.

TABLE 2.4
Sierra Leone—Estimated Fiscal Impact of Ebola in 2014 (as estimated on October 1, 2014)
US$ millions

	Pre-Ebola projection (a)	Revised projection (b)	Net change (b)–(a)	
Tax and non-tax revenue	580	522	–58	
Current expenditure	567	604	37	
Health response	0	26	26	
Social response	0	11	11	
Current balance net of adjustments	13	–82	–95	Pre-response fiscal impact
Capital expenditure	371	355	–16	
Grants	164	166	2	
Overall balance	–194	–271	–77	Net fiscal impact
Overall balance (% of GDP)	–4.2	–6.0	–1.8	

Source: World Bank and IMF estimates.

Guinea

Guinea is among the poorest countries in West Africa, with a population of 12 million and per capita income of US$460. It was the first country to be affected by the Ebola virus. When the epidemic hit, however, the Ministry of Health reacted swiftly, in partnership with Médecins Sans Frontières (MSF). Isolation wards were set up in Macenta and Gueckedou, the two most affected districts. Contact tracing and follow-up in these areas seem to have allowed the authorities to contain the epidemic, despite some recent cases of migration back from the border areas of Liberia and Sierra Leone.

The country is richly endowed with metals such as iron ore and bauxite and has strong hydro-power potential, but it is returning to macroeconomic and political stability after years of conflict and poor leadership. Its economy is a mix of agriculture, services, and mining. Recent income growth in Guinea has not matched that experienced by neighboring countries, and the poverty rate is high at over 55 percent of the population.

Impact on economic activity

The main economic impacts of Ebola in Guinea to date have been on agriculture and services. Projected agricultural growth for 2014 has been revised down from 5.7 percent to 3.3 percent. Agriculture in Ebola-affected areas has been hit by an exodus of people from these zones, affecting key export commodities such as cocoa and palm oil. Coffee production has also fallen by half (from 5,736 tons to 2,671 tons between the first six months of 2013 and the first six months of 2014); cocoa production has declined by a third (from 3,511 tons to 2,296 tons for the same time period). Palm oil production has fallen by 75 percent. Local water production has fallen by 29 percent.

Services have also been hit. Growth in services is projected to fall from 6.7 percent to 3.8 percent, with transport and commerce sub-sectors remaining stagnant. Services are, in part, tied to the mining sector, where major companies, including Vale and Rio Tinto, have evacuated many foreign workers. Airlines have reduced travel to Guinea, Senegal and Côte d'Ivoire have sealed their borders with the country, and many expatriates in the mining sector have left. Hotel occupancy rates in Conakry have fallen by half, to less than 40 percent, compared with an average occupancy of 80 percent before the crisis.

Still, mining output has not yet been severely affected by the Ebola outbreak, because the main mines are not located in the affected areas (with the exception of iron ore). For example, in the mining sector, where production was already forecast to contract by 3.0 percent before the Ebola outbreak, projected output has been revised downward to only 3.4 percent.

Manufacturing is a small sector in Guinea, accounting for less than 7 percent of GDP. It is mostly concentrated in Conakry, and includes agro-industry, paint, plastics, soft drinks, cement, and metals. The Ebola outbreak has made it more difficult for firms to obtain key imports due to port delays and logistics challenges. Cement imports have fallen by 50 percent year-to-date, relative to 2013.

The result of these sector effects are that projected GDP growth for 2014 has been revised from 4.5 percent to 2.4 percent (table 2.5).

Food prices and inflation

Price data until August suggest little effect to date of lower agricultural production on food prices in Guinea. Prices fell between April and June, with an uptick since July. Annual inflation for 2014 is still projected to be 8.5 percent (figure 2.13).

TABLE 2.5
Guinea—Estimated GDP Impact of Ebola (2014)
Percent

	Contribution to growth shock	Pre-Ebola projection (Jan 2014)	Revised projection
Real GDP growth	—	*4.5*	*2.4*
Agriculture	20.3	5.7	3.3
Forestry	0.0	3.5	3.5
Mining	3.8	–3.0	–3.4
Manufacturing	2.5	6.5	5.6
Services	73.5	6.7	3.8

Source: World Bank and IMF estimates.

External sector

There has been a slight trend of exchange rate depreciation (figure 2.14). According to the Central Bank, part of this is supply related as artisanal gold production is down. While this is in large part explained by seasonal fluctuations, Ebola is also contributing to capital flight as many expatriates (as well as some Guineans who can afford to) have left the country.

Fiscal impact

The fiscal impact of the Ebola outbreak on Guinea is estimated at US$120 million, of which US$50 million is attributed to revenue shortfalls and US$70 million to increased spending on the Ebola response (table 2.6). Lower revenues from mining sector royalties, taxes on international trade, and taxes on goods and services account for more than two-thirds of the revenue decline. The government has so far adopted a US$70 million response plan to fund logistics, health centers, food and equipment purchases, and salaries.

Neighboring Economies

So far, the Ebola epidemic has not had a major effect on economic activity outside the three core affected countries, although there have been some ripple effects. The first effect has been the movement of Ebola-infected

FIGURE 2.13
Guinea—Inflation and Food Prices (2014)

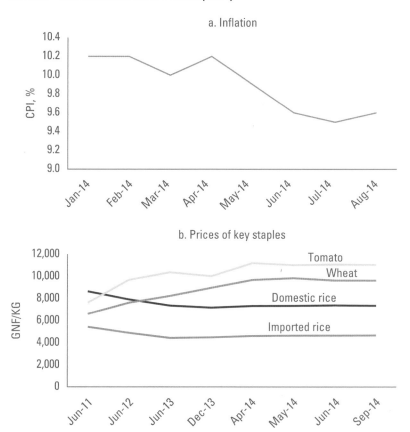

Source: World Bank calculations based on government data. CPI = consumer price index.

FIGURE 2.14
Guinea—US Dollar–Guinean Franc Nominal Exchange Rate (2014)

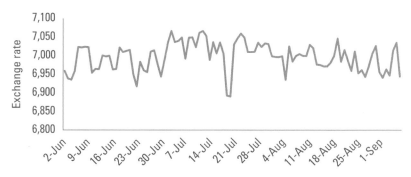

Source: World Bank calculations.

TABLE 2.6

Guinea—Estimated Fiscal Impact of Ebola in 2014 (as estimated on October 1, 2014)

US$ millions

	Pre-Ebola projection (a)	Revised projection (b)	Net change (b)–(a)	
Tax and non-tax revenue	1365	1315	–50	
Current expenditure	1090	1160	70	
Health response	0	50	50	
Social response	0	20	20	
Current balance net of adjustments	275	155	–120	Pre-response fiscal impact
Capital expenditure	870	870	0	
Grants	335	335	0	
Overall balance	–260	–380	–120	Net fiscal impact
Overall balance (% of GDP)	–4.0	–5.8	–1.8	

Source: World Bank and IMF estimates.

people from the core areas to Nigeria and Senegal. The arrival of the first cases in Nigeria and Senegal created a strong reaction among local populations, and the authorities took immediate measures to contain the infection (box 2.1). The second effect has been on cross-border trade as a result of borders being sealed. Both Côte d'Ivoire and Senegal initially sealed their borders with Guinea, and other countries have made movements in the same direction. This affects the trade flows between these countries. Additional channels of economic transmission may yet appear, although countries in the region are making medical preparations to reduce that risk.

Nigeria

The emergence of Ebola in Nigeria, followed by a successful containment effort, likely had a very modest economic impact. Preliminary reports from shopping centers and many commercial businesses in Lagos, following initial emergence of the virus, indicated significant declines in demand, sometimes in the range of 20–40 percent. However, the government spent significant resources on containment, successfully stemming the epidemic (box 2.1). The early decline in commerce likely reflected initial shock, fear, and uncertainty following the appearance of

Ebola in Lagos and Port Harcourt. Confidence around what was a successful containment effort should have returned commerce to near-normal levels. While even the successfully contained outbreak of Ebola in Nigeria may discourage foreign tourists from visiting the country, Nigeria has a relatively small foreign tourist industry to begin with, so the effect will be marginal. Nigeria's high dependence on oil to fund exports and provide budgetary resources may actually be an advantage in the face of any Ebola outbreak, as the oil sector is highly regionally concentrated with much activity located offshore, and should not suffer Ebola-related disruptions in the absence of a mass epidemic. Official trade flows with West Africa are relatively small. Informal trade flows are much larger, although it is not clear how these flows would be affected by any Ebola-related trade disruptions. GDP growth in Nigeria is expected to be close to 6 percent in 2014, and the general government budget is expected to be close to balanced.

Côte d'Ivoire

So far, Côte d'Ivoire has been spared any Ebola outbreak, and the government has taken measures to limit the risks of contagion from neighboring Guinea, Liberia, and Sierra Leone. These measures include closing the borders with Liberia and Guinea for over a month and imposing mandatory health checks on all visitors, as well as implementing an intensive public sensitization campaign. Notwithstanding these measures, concerns regarding Côte d'Ivoire's exposure to Ebola remain, owing to the porousness of borders and the often free circulation of the population across them, including in areas affected by the Ebola outbreak in Liberia and Guinea.

Guinea-Bissau

No cases of Ebola have yet been reported in Guinea-Bissau. To protect its citizens from the spread of the disease, the government closed the border with Guinea in August. Guinea-Bissau is poorly integrated in regional trade networks so the economic effect is likely to be marginal. Health professionals have warned closing the border might in fact be counter-productive, by diverting travelers to unofficial, porous border crossings and thus reducing the authorities' ability to monitor the cross-border traffic of potential Ebola victims. A weak health sector in the country reduces the authorities' ability to both identify and treat Ebola cases. The World Bank is thus restructuring an ongoing Community Driven Development project to make US$750,000 available to the WHO to enhance the country's medical preparedness. The project will also support a campaign to raise awareness of Ebola and of prevention mechanisms. Assuming that Guinea-Bissau avoids Ebola, the estimate for 2014 growth remains unchanged at 3 percent, with an expected fiscal deficit of 1.7 percent of GDP.

Senegal and the Gambia

The one confirmed case of Ebola in Senegal has been successfully treated (box 2.1), and the economic impact on Senegal so far is modest. Recent economic indicators are nearly in line with the pre-Ebola GDP growth projection of 4.9 percent for 2014. Based on the index of general activity (excluding agriculture), GDP growth is estimated at 4.7 percent for the first two quarters of 2014, driven mainly by services (up 6.6 percent) and public administration (up 7.3 percent). However, delay in the onset of the rainy season and the outbreak of Ebola could result in a slowdown in growth for the remainder of the year. Senegal had previously closed its border with Guinea in an attempt to halt the spread of Ebola and had banned flights and ships from Guinea, Liberia, and Sierra Leone. Exports to these countries only account for 2 percent of total Senegalese exports, so the effects of these transport limitations will be small.

The impact of Ebola on tourism will be more important. Tourism is the largest single foreign exchange earner, accounting for some 12 percent of total exports of goods and services. If tourism falls by half, this would lead to a 1 percent drop in GDP on an annual basis. Several conferences have already been canceled and incoming flights have relatively few passengers. There are no available data on tourist flows in Senegal, but in neighboring Gambia which is one of the larger tourism markets in West Africa, tourism is a key economic sector. Direct receipts from tourism are 11.4 percent of GDP, and it is an important economic sector for direct and indirect employment, with many linkages to other services. Moreover, it is a significant contributor to government revenue.

Since the onset of the Ebola crisis in Liberia, Sierra Leone, and Guinea, it was estimated that 65 percent of hotel reservations in the Gambia had already been canceled, which will have a profound impact on the economy. Should the crisis persist, there may be second-round effects through the deferral or cancellation of FDI, most of which is tied to tourism or the hospitality sector more broadly, and which has been averaging nearly 7 percent of GDP annually. The situation will be seriously aggravated if the disease spreads to Mali beyond the single case in late October, since this is Senegal's number one export destination as well as the most important client for transit trade. There are already additional public expenses related to the funding of emergency

BOX 2.1
Containing the Epidemic in Senegal and Nigeria

As the number of cases mounts in Guinea, Liberia, and Sierra Leone, concern continues that the epidemic could spread further across the region and beyond. Two countries in the region have experienced one or more cases but have successfully contained the epidemic.

Senegal

In late August, a single case was reported in Senegal. The patient was a Guinean national who had traveled by road to Dakar. The Ministry of Health in Senegal, with support from the World Health Organization, Médecins Sans Frontières, and the U.S. Centers for Disease Control, identified the disease and carried out swift and effective contact tracing. As of two weeks after the case had been initially diagnosed, 67 close contacts of the patient had been identified and were monitored twice daily. Two of those contacts had developed symptoms and were tested, but the results were negative. Three additional cases across the country had been tested and were found to be negative. As of early October, no additional cases had been identified. The single positive case fully recovered and was discharged.[a]

Estimates put the costs of treatment and contact tracing at close to US$1 million. Senegal and partners have invested approximately US$2 million more in laboratory and facility strengthening, as well as close to US$3 million for surveillance, community outreach, and coordination of these efforts.[b]

Nigeria

A single case arrived by air in Lagos in mid-July. The Ministry of Health, again with support from partners, carried out effective contact tracing. One infected contact traveled to Port Harcourt (Rivers State) for treatment, leading to several additional cases. Ultimately, 15 cases were confirmed in Lagos and 4 were confirmed in Rivers. For those 19 cases, 890 contacts were listed and all but one completed a 21-day follow up. No new cases have been documented. Across the two states, the government of Nigeria allocated roughly US$13 million in direct costs. Moreover, the effectiveness of the effort is attributed to strong federal-state partnerships, and strong government-donor partnerships.[c]

In both countries, the price tag has been high in terms of treatment, contact tracing, and enhancing surveillance systems and community outreach. But based on the massive estimated economic cost of the large-scale outbreaks in other countries with much smaller economies, these are resources very well spent.

Source: World Bank, based on data provided by the World Bank country teams for Senegal and Nigeria.
a. Information on the outbreak and the response come from WHO (2014c) and WHO (2014d).
b. Data on costs come from World Bank calculations.
c. Data on the outbreak are from WHO (2014d) and the Nigerian Ministry of Health. Costs are World Bank calculations.

TABLE 2.7
Forgone GDP Due to Ebola in Three Most Affected Countries (2014)
US$ millions

Country	Projected GDP 2014 (no Ebola)	Projected GDP 2014 (with Ebola)	Forgone GDP
Liberia	2,066	2,000	66
Sierra Leone	5,486	5,324	163
Guinea	6,471	6,341	130

Source: World Bank calculations.
Note: All numbers are in 2013 dollars.

measures put in place, notably through the Ministry of Health, but donors appear ready to cover most of these costs.

Conclusion

Preliminary estimates for 2014 indicate that GDP growth could be halved in Guinea and Liberia, with a loss of 3 percentage points for Sierra Leone. In terms of foregone output, this amounts to a total of US$359 million across the three countries, already a major loss (table 2.7).

The fiscal impact of the crisis on the core three countries has been enormous, emanating from revenue shortfalls due to reduced economic activities, combined with increased expenditures on health, security, and social protection. The 2014 financing gaps for the three core countries range from US$80 million to US$120 million, summing to over US$290 million. Slow containment and continued exponential growth of the disease will lead to even greater financing gaps in 2015.

Medium-Term Impacts

If the Ebola epidemic were contained over the course of 2014, future economic impacts would be lessened, as individuals and institutions could begin to recover and catch up relatively quickly. However, some impacts—including losses in human capital due to interrupted schooling and reduced household wealth—may have significant long-run repercussions. Perhaps more important, most epidemiological projections now suggest that the epidemic will in fact continue into 2015. This section presents estimates for the medium run, through the end of 2015, for the three countries at the core of the crisis and for West Africa as a whole.

Methods of Estimation

In order to provide estimates on both the three core affected countries and West Africa, a number of approaches were used; the relationship between the methods is summarized in figure 3.1. To estimate medium-term impacts on the individual countries, this report employs the same method as that for the short-term estimates: using available data on the ground to estimate the change in projected growth rates by sector and then combining those—weighted by the relative share of each sector in the economy—to calculate the updated change in the growth rate.[7] For one country, Liberia, a dynamic computable general equilibrium (CGE) model, based on a detailed Liberian database, was available for immediate implementation; this made it possible to provide additional insights, drawing on the Liberia-specific projected change in growth rates to make reasonable adjustments to capital, labor, and transaction costs and then calculate the likely impact of the epidemic on poverty.

The specific CGE model is the Maquette for Millenium Development Goal Simulations (MAMS).[8] The advantage of a model of this type is that

FIGURE 3.1
Relationship across Models

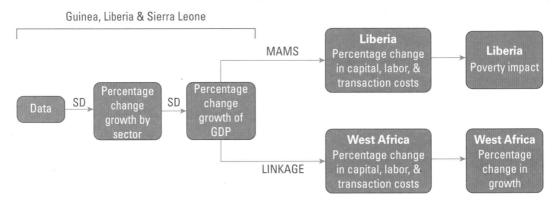

Note: SD = sector decomposition method; MAMS = Liberia-specific CGE model; LINKAGE = global CGE model.

it imposes basic economic mechanisms, including markets with flexible prices and the constraints and linkages that are important in any economy. Employment of labor, capital, and other factors is limited to what is available. Production in one sector generates demands for the outputs of downstream sectors and meets the demands of upstream sectors, households, investors, and exporters. Private and government incomes are affected by government policies, production, foreign trade, and donor aid. The spending of the nation as a whole and for each type of agent (the government, firms, and households) must be fully financed by some combination of current incomes, grants, and net borrowing, some of which may come from abroad.

CGE modeling also permits the estimation of the impact of the Ebola epidemic on West Africa more generally, capturing the spillover and feedback effects across economies. For this purpose, this report employs the LINKAGE model, which draws on the Global Trade Analysis Project (GTAP) database of economic transactions within and across economies for 2013.[9] For this implementation of LINKAGE, all the countries in the world are grouped into 12 region/country aggregates, 6 of which are within Sub-Saharan Africa.[10] Aggregating the LINKAGE results for the economies of Nigeria, Ghana, Senegal, and a "rest of West Africa" group provides an estimate of the impact of Ebola on West Africa as a whole. Because the three core affected countries represent only about 11 percent of the GDP of the "rest of West Africa" aggregate, it is not possible to separate an estimate for the impact of the crisis for the three core countries from the estimate for the aggregate using the LINKAGE model.

For this reason, the medium-term projections rely on a sectoral decomposition method for the core country estimates, complemented by MAMS for Liberia and the LINKAGE model for overall West Africa impacts.

Scenarios of the Ebola Epidemic

In late August 2014, WHO proposed that "the aggregate case load of EVD could exceed 20,000 over the course of this emergency" (WHO 2014b). Newer projections have suggested a much larger potential caseload and—importantly—a *longer* epidemic (Grady 2014).[11] For example, without a significant course correction, the U.S. Centers for Disease Control and Prevention (CDC) puts the total caseload in those two countries at above one million by the end of January 2015 (Meltzer et al. 2014). Revised numbers from the WHO suggest a caseload of 20,000 by the beginning of November (WHO Ebola Response Team 2014). Given the highly volatile situation, with new information appearing almost on a daily basis, the focus here is not on generating point estimates of expected effects. Rather, we use multiple approaches to assess the consequences of alternative epidemiological and economic trajectories on different indicators, including production (measured by GDP), public spending and revenues, as well as, when possible, poverty. To capture the range of plausible outcomes, two scenarios for the three most affected countries capture—first—relatively rapid Ebola containment with limited spread to other countries and—second—relatively slow Ebola containment with more spread to other countries.

Under the more rapid containment scenario (called Low Ebola), the caseload reaches around 20,000, with containment of the disease achieved by roughly the end of 2014—through the first quarter of 2015 at the latest—and a broad resumption of economic activity in 2015. Under the slow containment scenario (High Ebola), the number of cases is much higher, reaching around 200,000, with increases in late 2014 and the beginning of 2015 before the outbreak is brought under control in the middle of 2015.[12] This analysis does not incorporate the U.S. Centers for Disease Control's estimate of 1.4 million cases (Meltzer et al. 2014) for two reasons. First, while aversion behavior increases with the number of cases, it does not increase linearly: A caseload in the hundreds of thousands is already likely to dramatically reduce investment, especially by foreign investors, and an increase beyond that may not have a major impact. Second, the 1.4 million case estimate assumes no "additional interventions or changes in community behavior." There is already evidence of changing community behavior and additional interventions at national and international levels.

Estimates of the Impact of Ebola

Liberia

Drawing on the sector decomposition method and expert assessments, our analysis suggests that, if Ebola is contained within the next six months or so—a Low Ebola case—economic activity may gradually increase across most sectors, enabling the Liberian economy to post a modest rebound in 2015, with GDP growth of about 2.6 percent. Such growth is expected to be driven mainly by the more resilient iron ore mining sector, agriculture, and services including construction (particularly residential construction, which may be more easily mobilized). Even with the rebound, prices (food prices in particular) may remain sticky and exchange rate volatility may persist into 2015.

If the epidemic is not so rapidly contained, economic reactions driven by fear may be heightened, precipitating further economic shocks that could shut down production in large-scale mines and further delay investments in capacity expansion. Other likely effects are further disruption to regional and international flights; interruption of the 2015 planting seasons for the two main staples, rice and cassava; and the shut-down of borders and markets. Financial markets and international trade would be affected. Under this slow containment scenario, the sharp contraction in agriculture, manufacturing and services, as well as the cessation of mining would lead to an overall GDP contraction of nearly 5 percent (table 3.1), and a loss of US$228 million in output (in 2013 dollars). Under such a High Ebola scenario, the sharp reduction in economic activities would result in substantial fall-out in fiscal revenues, pushing the fiscal gap well beyond the current estimate of nearly US$100 million.

TABLE 3.1
Liberia—Estimated GDP Impact of Ebola (2015)

	Annual growth rates			
	2012	**2013**	**2014**	**2015**
Pre-crisis baseline GDP	8.3	8.7	5.9	6.8
GDP with Ebola	—	—	2.5	Low Ebola: 1.0 High Ebola: –5.2

Liberia—CGE results

In the case of Liberia, we complement the sector decomposition results with analysis using MAMS. (The assumptions and results of the MAMS analysis are laid out in more detail in appendix D.) Two scenarios are assessed, a Low Ebola scenario with fewer cases due to a relatively stronger government response in 2014, and a High Ebola scenario with more cases (over a longer time) due to a weaker government response in 2014. For each scenario, we develop a set of shocks to transactions, input coefficients, and factor supplies. For the Low Ebola case, the assumptions generate outcomes that, in terms of GDP (i.e., production) changes, are quite close to those generated by the sector decomposition method. However, given that the methods are distinct, the results are not identical. For the High Ebola case, the assumptions are designed to explore the impact of a more severe (but still plausible) Ebola trajectory with a serious deterioration during the remaining months of 2014 before new cases come to an end during 2015.

Given these assumptions, the results of these simulations permit us to highlight how Liberia's economy reaches different outcomes under the Low and High Ebola cases. As shown in figure 3.2 for Low Ebola, total real GDP at factor cost (a measure of the quantity of production) declines compared to the baseline scenario during 2014 but returns to close to baseline levels in 2015, thanks to a significant growth catch-up as labor and other factor inputs that were underutilized in 2014 return

FIGURE 3.2
Liberia—Real GDP at Factor Cost (2013–15)

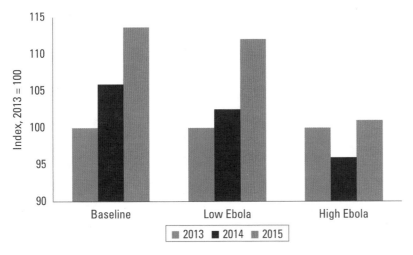

to production, and Ebola-related impediments to domestic and foreign trade vanish. By contrast, for High Ebola, a severe worsening of the crisis toward the end of 2014 leads to severe factor underutilization, trade obstacles and other negative repercussions; in 2015, the crisis remains severe. As a result, real GDP losses during 2014 are more severe, and in 2015 the GDP gap between High Ebola and the two other scenarios increases further.

The impact on per capita household consumption is more severe than indicated by the GDP figures—one significant consequence of the Ebola-related interruption of trade is severe efficiency losses, reflected in increasing wedges between consumer and producer prices, which reduce consumer purchasing power. Without Ebola, some 55–60 percent of the population lives under the national poverty line. Furthermore, many households live close to the poverty line, so even a small shock can plunge them into poverty. As a result, the decline in household consumption under Ebola is reflected by a strong increase in poverty.[13] The results are summarized in figure 3.3. In the Low Ebola scenario, the headcount poverty rate jumps from 57 percent in 2013 to 67 percent in 2014, although it returns to pre-Ebola and baseline levels in 2015: Rapid response and containment can limit the poverty impact. However, in the High Ebola scenario, the headcount poverty rate jumps even higher in 2014 and continues to increase in 2015, reaching 75 percent, i.e. an increase of 18 percentage points over already high levels in 2013. Beyond the mortal tragedy that is Ebola, there is the potential of a further tragedy, as poverty levels increase dramatically among the survivors.

FIGURE 3.3
Headcount Poverty Rate under Alternative Scenarios (2013–15)

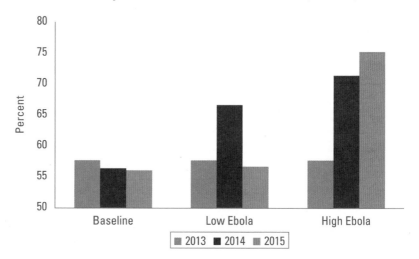

Sierra Leone

Sierra Leone's overall growth prospects are dominated by the iron ore sub-sector, the mainstay of its mining sector. A positive aspect of this is that as the still fledgling iron ore industry expands, it increases overall GDP significantly. However, such an enclave sector, which has few linkages to the rest of the economy, can mask the performance of other sectors in the economy. Thus GDP numbers for Sierra Leone are broken out for non-iron ore GDP (table 3.2). Under the assumption that the Ebola outbreak is contained relatively quickly (Low Ebola), an economic recovery emerges over the course of 2015, anchored by government spending and iron ore, which increases production rapidly after the end of the crisis. Agricultural growth falls to just over 2 percent as the effects of missing the planting season in 2014 appear through a weak harvest. The service sector rebounds, led by manufacturing and the return of tourism and foreign visitors. Under this scenario, non-iron ore GDP rises by 4.5 percent in 2015. Overall GDP rises by 7.7 percent relative to 8.9 percent in the pre-crisis projections, representing a loss of approximately US\$59 million (in 2013 dollars).

A more pessimistic, slow-containment scenario is also simulated (High Ebola), built on the assumption that efforts to end the crisis will not bear fruit until well into 2015. Under this assumption, agricultural output falls dramatically due to large-scale abandonment by farmers and rural deaths. Food crop and cash crop production fall, necessitating increased imports, which—coupled with widespread shortages—place pressure on inflation and the exchange rate. Services also contract, especially for the hospitality sector. Only government spending buoys the economy. The major mines are assumed to be shut for at least half the year. Under these assumptions, overall economic

TABLE 3.2
Sierra Leone—Estimated GDP Impact of Ebola (2015)

	Annual growth rates			
	2012	**2013**	**2014**	**2015**
Pre-crisis baseline GDP	15.2	20.1	11.3	8.9
Non-iron ore GDP	5.3	5.5	6.0	6.3
GDP with Ebola	—	—	8.0	Low Ebola: 7.7 High Ebola: 0.0
Non-iron ore GDP	—	—	4.0	Low Ebola: 4.5 High Ebola: −3.0

Source: World Bank estimates.

growth is zero in 2015 and the non-iron ore economy shrinks by 3 percent. The ensuing post-crisis recovery would be expected to be slow, with growth shrinking to zero in 2015; this is associated with US$439 million in lost GDP, more than seven times the loss in the Low Ebola scenario.

Guinea

Absent any further outbreak of disease in Guinea, the economy is projected to remain resilient in the medium term, propelled by a rebound in services and stronger mining performance. The impact of Ebola will still be felt in 2015, even assuming an optimistic six-to-nine month crisis response operation. But estimates of Guinea's projected GDP growth in 2015 span a much narrower range than those described above for Liberia and Sierra Leone, from 2 percent to 5 percent, given the containment of the outbreak in Guinea (table 3.3). The Low Ebola scenario actually represents an increase relative to the pre-crisis projections, but the High Ebola scenario results in a loss of US$142 million in output (in 2013 dollars). There nonetheless remains the risk of Ebola affecting Guinea's mining sector, which would lead to a dramatic departure of business and FDI at a time when the country needs international support. An additional danger is that negative perceptions associated with Ebola linger even after the situation on the ground has improved.

West Africa

The shocks to transaction costs (both domestic and international), to labor force participation, and to capital utilization are assumed to be at their worst in Liberia. Those shocks were backed out of the sector

TABLE 3.3
Guinea—Estimated GDP Impact of Ebola (2015)

	Annual growth rates			
	2012	**2013**	**2014**	**2015**
Pre-crisis baseline GDP	3.8	2.3	4.5	4.3
GDP with Ebola	—	—	2.4	Low Ebola: 5.0 High Ebola: 2.0

Source: World Bank estimates.

decomposition estimates for Liberia and subsequently applied in the Liberia-specific CGE model (MAMS). In order to estimate the impact of the Ebola epidemic for West Africa, those shocks to transaction costs and factor inputs are scaled down for other countries in the region and around the world and then incorporated into the LINKAGE model.

In order to scale the level of the shocks in other countries, an "Ebola impact index" is constructed, based on two attributes of each country. The first attribute is the size of a potential Ebola outbreak: This potential outbreak size is calculated using the likelihood of a single case arriving in a given country, multiplied by the number of cases likely to emerge once a single case breaks out. The second attribute is the country's GDP, a proxy for the quality of the health-care system.[14] The likelihood of a single case and the likely number of cases were estimated using airplane flight patterns in a recent paper by Gomes et al. (2014). Of course, flights are not the only way that Ebola travels: The patient who arrived in Nigeria came by flight, but the patient who arrived in Senegal came by land. However, flight patterns serve as one useful, albeit imperfect, proxy for the likely spread of the epidemic. Both the likelihood of a single case and the likely number of cases have low and high scenarios, which we convert into a Low Ebola scenario (with relatively little spread) and a High Ebola scenario (with much more spread). The precise calculations are detailed in appendix B. Figure 3.4 displays a scatter plot of the "Ebola Impact Index" against a country's GDP. Note the log scale, which indicates that the probability of an outbreak in richer countries with fewer direct flight connections to affected countries is very low, and even neighbor countries have dramatically lower expected impacts than the three most affected countries. The countries with the highest impact index will not necessarily get an Ebola case, nor will they necessarily greatly suffer if they do. However, the Ebola Impact Index does suggest which countries are in greatest danger of potential infection.[15]

The LINKAGE model uses these Ebola Impact Index values to scale down the perturbations (in transaction costs and factor levels) that we assume are introduced because of aversion behavior. By virtue of both their GDP and their relatively few links by air with Liberia, Sierra Leone, and Guinea, the United States and Germany are not predicted to bear a large Ebola burden. But all the West African countries are at risk to one degree or another. Building on the assumptions in Gomes et al. (2014), we model the six countries or country groupings[16] most likely to have an Ebola case, assuming the disease does not travel beyond those.

The inputs to the LINKAGE model in terms of reductions in labor, capital utilization, and trade and transaction margins for the West Africa region are as illustrated in table 3.4. All of those inputs are scaled from the effects in Liberia, according to the probability of having a case and

FIGURE 3.4
Ebola Impact Index and National GDP under the Low Ebola Scenario

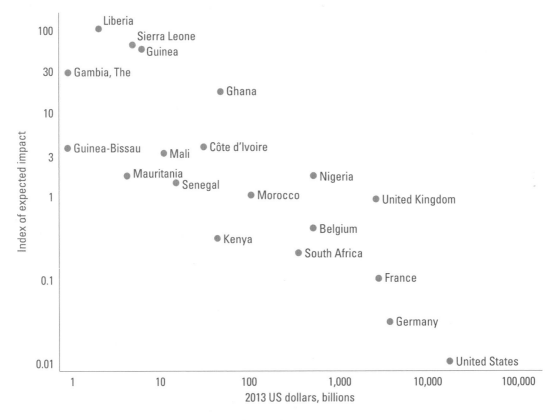

Source: World Bank, based on World Development Indicators 2013.

the likely number of cases, per Gomes et al. (2014) using the Ebola impact index.

The result is that, in the Low Ebola case, there is quite a modest difference in economic growth for West Africa as a whole for the year 2015 (table 3.5). The average growth over the course of 2014–15 would be lower because growth takes a significant hit for the three core countries in 2014 and a much smaller hit for other countries in the region. But with swift, effective action, the regional economic impact of the crisis could be contained. However, in the High Ebola case, the economic impact is much more dire. With a large expansion of the outbreak and Ebola spreading to some other countries within the region, there is a more significant reduction in labor and capital utilization. In addition, transaction costs increase by a further 3 percentage points, and the impact on exports and imports is much more significant. Export growth would be more than 5 percentage points lower in 2014 in the High Ebola scenario compared to the baseline. Exports recover in 2015, but their

TABLE 3.4
Assumptions about Changes in Factor Availability in the West Africa Region as Compared with the Baseline (2014–15)
Percent

Variables	Baseline		Low Ebola		High Ebola	
	2014	2015	2014	2015	2014	2015
Labor force growth rates	2.3	2.3	2.2	2.3	1.7	0.9
Capital utilization	100	100	99.2	99.9	97.7	95.6
Trade and transaction margins[a]	100	100	102	100	105	110

Source: World Bank projections based on LINKAGE model.
a. International trade and domestic transaction margins. The increase in trade and transaction margins shown above refers to the Rest of West Africa regional aggregate, while the impacts are scaled for Ghana, Senegal, and Nigeria, as well as other regions.

TABLE 3.5
Annual GDP Growth Rates of the West Africa Region in the Baseline and the Low Ebola and High Ebola Scenarios (2013–15)
Percent

	(1)	(2)	(3)	(4)	(5)	(6)	(7)
		Baseline		Low Ebola		High Ebola	
Variables	2013	2014	2015	2014	2015	2014	2015
Investment	100	107.7	117.5	107.6	120.6	104.4	106.3
Price of exports[a]	100	100	100	98.5	100	96.4	93.1
Exports	100	109.6	119.3	107.6	119.2	104.0	105.7
GDP volume	100	106.7	113.5	106.4	113.3	105.6	109.9
GDP annual growth rates	6.9	6.7	6.4	6.4	6.5	5.6	4.1
GDP (2013 USD billion)	709.3	756.6	805.2	754.4	803.5	749.3	779.9
GDP lost (USD billion)	—	—	—	2.2	1.6	7.4	25.2

Source: World Bank projections based on LINKAGE model.
Note: Dollar figures are in 2013 US dollars.
a. Price of exports net of transaction costs.

volume remains significantly below their baseline value in 2014. The GDP growth rate declines to 4.1 percent in 2014. This is the GDP growth rate for the West Africa region as a whole, which indicates that for the countries most affected by the Ebola outbreak, the economic decline is likely to be much more significant.

The resulting slower growth rate leads to a loss of output worth US$7.35 billion in 2014. Output continues to grow at a much slower pace in 2015 than in the baseline case, leading to a further loss of US$25.2 billion.[17] Overall, in the High Ebola scenario, the GDP of West Africa is only 10 percent higher than its 2013 level by the end of 2015, while in the absence of Ebola it would have been 19 percent higher (see table 3.5, columns 3 and 7). In addition to the immeasurable costs of lives lost, the loss of income in the High Ebola scenario could take years to recover.

Taking the two years together, this translates into a moderate loss in GDP volume in the Low Ebola case: The lost GDP amounts to US$3.8 billion by the end of 2015 (2013 dollars). But in the High Ebola case, the loss in GDP reaches almost nine times that, at about US$32.6 billion over the two years (figure 3.5). That is 4.10 percent of what regional GDP would have been in the absence of Ebola in 2014. This is an enormous cost, not only for the most affected countries, but also for the region as a whole. It has the potential to be deeply desta- bilizing and requires an immediate response.

FIGURE 3.5
Impact of Ebola on GDP and Annual Growth Rates for West Africa (2013–15)

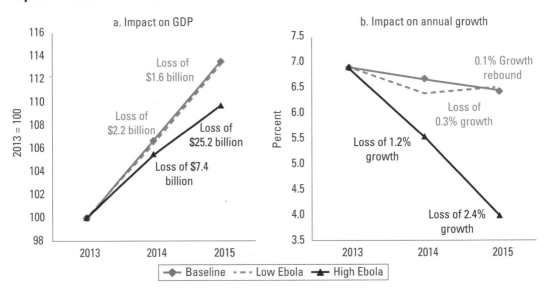

Source: World Bank calculations.

FIGURE 3.6
Lost GDP Due to Ebola over the Short and Medium Run

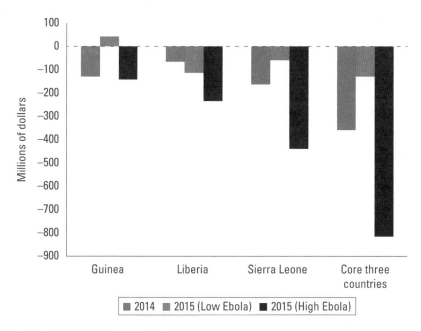

Note: Estimates are in 2013 US dollars.

Conclusion

For the three core countries, the forfeited GDP in 2015 sums to US$129 million in the Low Ebola case and a striking US$815 million in the High Ebola case (2013 dollars). As figure 3.6 demonstrates, the likely economic impact of the Ebola epidemic will be significant for the affected countries in any plausible scenario. However, the case in which the epidemic is not swiftly contained threatens to leave a much deeper economic scar, with billions of dollars in lost revenue in either scenario.

Concluding Remarks

Diseases and the pain and suffering they cause engender treatment costs as well as the costs of reduced productivity. At the time of writing, more than 5,000 people have died in Liberia, Sierra Leone, and Guinea alone, with some experts placing the true number two or three times higher. Cases continue to accumulate in all three countries (WHO 2014a).

A correct primary focus is on containment, treating the ill, and helping relatives and communities to recover. However, there will also be a need over time to help the affected countries in their post-Ebola economic recovery. The magnitude of the estimated impacts demonstrates the need for a concerted international response. While it is beyond the scope of this paper to assess how much donor funding is needed either to aid the health sectors of African countries, or to return their economies to robust economic growth, abating the aversion behavior that causes most of the economic impact will require at least the following four related sets of activities.

Containing the Epidemic

It is clear that the aversion behavior in any individual country, and in the world at large, will persist until public health interventions have reversed the growth of Ebola cases in Liberia, Sierra Leone, and Guinea and have demonstrated their competence in rapidly containing each newly discovered case in any other country. The estimates of immediate humanitarian costs from WHO and the United Nations have been revised upward, from US$495 to US$600 million (Clarke and Samb 2014). These amounts will finance desperately needed personal protective equipment for health workers, emergency treatment units, salaries, and so on and are required just to shore up the ongoing efforts to contain the epidemic. The World Bank is working with affected countries and other donors to re-program existing money and channel new grant funding in order to procure the needed supplies as quickly as possible. These expenditures, if they prove effective, will lay the groundwork for other policies to further allay the apprehension of economic agents, thus providing the initial conditions for reviving economic growth.

Fiscal Support

The robust economic growth anticipated for the three core countries for 2014 and 2015 is rapidly becoming elusive. Increased injections of external support can enable these governments to continue to function as growth resumes in these fragile economies. The fiscal gap, just for 2014, is estimated at around US$290 million. In either scenario, but especially in the more pessimistic scenario, that is likely to be much, much higher. This represents not the price tag of mitigating the economic impact, but merely the cost of keeping governments running and providing services as they and their partners continue to fight the epidemic.

Restoring Investor Confidence

A key issue looking forward will be to re-establish investor trust so that as the epidemic is contained, domestic and international investment can return. There is an urgent need for policies that enable the flow of relief and encourage commercial exchange (for health, business, and tourism purposes) with the affected countries, while also safeguarding partners from epidemiological contagion. To this end, options should be explored for financing improvements to health security infrastructure and to seaport and airport protocols in the three core countries and their neighbors.

Strengthening the Surveillance, Detection, and Treatment Capacity of African Health Systems

Today, the governments of West African countries and their partners are fighting to control the Ebola outbreak. But effort and memory will be required to sustain and continue investing in effective and resilient African health systems—including epidemiological surveillance—after the Ebola outbreak has been contained.[18]

Starting now, the international community must learn and act on the knowledge that weak public health infrastructure, institutions, and systems in many African countries are a threat not only to their own citizens, but also to their trading partners and the world at large. The enormous economic cost of the current outbreak to the affected countries and the world could likely have been avoided by prudent ongoing investment in such health system strengthening. The Ebola outbreak has laid bare the failure of any reasoning that investments in public health infrastructure, institutions, and systems can be separated from investments in economic recovery and development. Building the infrastructure, institutions, and systems necessary to prevent future outbreaks (of Ebola or other pathogens) confers benefits that are non-rival and non-excludable.

Taken together, the containment effort, fiscal support, restoration of investor confidence, and expanded disease surveillance, diagnostic, and treatment capacity promise to first stem the Ebola epidemic, and then to help reverse as quickly as possible the aversion behavior that is causing so much economic damage. Quick action by the international community working in concert with the directly affected governments is crucial to avert a regional and global calamity.

Sector Decomposition of GDP

The projections of GDP growth in this report involved the decomposition of GDP growth into sector components from the production side, based on 2014 sector weights and an assessment of the impact of the Ebola shock on the growth of each sector, based on a body of micro-economic evidence obtained in each country. (See the estimates of sector size and growth rates for Liberia and Sierra Leone in tables A.1 and A.2., respectively) The same methodology was applied across the three countries.

Representatives of economic sectors were contacted to assess changes in economic activity. For example, mining officials provided metrics of the extent to which Ebola was affecting production plans. These metrics were, in turn, based on recently revised plans by the operators of major mines. The projections were also informed by leading indicators that are usually good predictors of economic activity. Cement imports and sales were used to project the impact of Ebola on construction activity and thereby on services. Data on agricultural exports, as well as information regarding the stage(s) of the crop cycle interrupted by the crisis, were used to estimate agricultural production shocks. Hotel occupancy rates, airline traffic, and fuel sales volumes provided metrics for the transport and tourism sub-sectors. Possible effects on the exchange rate and on the import bill have not been assessed owing to the lack of a (counterfactual) baseline for comparison, but these data are nonetheless reported in the text. In all cases, projections reflecting the impact (to date) of Ebola were compared with pre-Ebola projections done by World Bank and IMF staff.

The assessments noted above, which also included information from government economic and statistical agencies, consistently suggested that growth in the first half of 2014 had been on track. The revised growth

TABLE A.1
Estimation of Revised Country-Level GDP for Liberia (2014)
Percentages

Projection for 2014, by sector	Sector share	Annualized growth		Overall growth
		First half 2014 (pre-Ebola)	Second half 2014 (with Ebola)	
Real GDP	*100.0*	*5.9*	*−0.7*	*2.5*
Agriculture	**24.5**	**3.5**	**−0.8**	**1.3**
Rubber	2.6	0.0	−9.7	−5.0[a]
Rice	6.6	3.5	−3.3	0.0[b]
Cassava	6.8	3.5	−1.5	1.0[b]
Forestry	**9.8**	**2.0**	**2.0**	**2.0**
Mining and quarrying	**13.2**	**4.4**	**−6.6**	**−1.3**
Iron ore	11.8	4.5	−8.6	−2.3[c]
Manufacturing	**7.5**	**9.6**	**0.6**	**5.0**
Cement	1.6	17.0	9.1	13.0
Beverages and beer	5.4	8.0	−1.7	3.0[d]
Other	0.5	5.0	−1.0	2.0
Services sector	**45.0**	**8.1**	**0.1**	**4.0**
Construction	4.9	24.0	2.9	13.0
Trade, hotels, etc.	14.1	7.0	−2.7	2.0
Transportation and communication	5.1	8.0	−3.6	2.0[e]
Financial institutions	3.2	2.8	1.2	2.0
Government services	7.1	10.0	6.0	8.0

Source: World Bank and IMF estimates.
a. Ongoing low-price supply response exacerbated by withdrawal of labor due to Ebola crisis.
b. Abandonment of farms.
c. Closure of China Union operations and departure of expatriates from gold and diamond mining operation.
d. Lower demand for beverages and beer from the slowdown in the hotel sector, resulting from the suspension of flights.
e. Impact on the transport sector seen from the sharp decline in the volume of diesel.

rates are therefore a weighted average of the initially projected rates for the first half of the year and adjusted growth rates for the second half.

The 2015 projections are based on the same approach for the two scenarios elaborated in the main text; the estimates for Liberia and Sierra Leone are presented in tables A.3 and A.4, respectively. The degree of uncertainty surrounding these is commensurately higher.

TABLE A.2
Estimation of Revised Country-Level GDP for Sierra Leone (2014)
Percentages

Projection for 2014, by sector	Sector share	Annualized growth		Overall growth
		First half 2014 (pre-Ebola)	Second half 2014 (with Ebola)	
Real GDP	*93.7*	*11.3*	*1.4*	*8.0*
Agriculture forestry, fisheries	**42.3**	**4.8**	**0.9**	**2.8**
Rice and other food crops	28.8	5.7	1.0	3.2[a]
Cash crops, livestock, forestry	7.7	3.6	0.8	2.2
Fisheries	5.8	1.9	0.6	1.9
Industry	**28.1**	**24.9**	**1.9**	**18.0**
Iron ore	20.9	31.5	2.0	23.0[b]
Other mining	3.1	−0.9	−1.0	−0.1[c]
Other industry	4.1	10.8	1.4	6.4
Services	**23.3**	**7.7**	**1.2**	**5.7**
Trade and tourism	7.5	12.0	1.4	6.0[d]
Transport, storage, communication	6.5	7.7	1.2	5.0[e]
Government services	9.2	5.7	1.0	7.6[f]

Source: World Bank and IMF estimates.
a. Rice and food crops largely harvested in 2014.
b. Iron ore production falls in H2 due to low world prices and higher shipping and insurance.
c. Falling diamond production influencing this.
d. Slow growth in H2 on account of imports related to emergency.
e. Falling fuel sales recover in H2 due to relief effort.
f. Increased public expenditures on health and general public administration.

TABLE A.3
GDP Scenarios for Liberia (2015)
Percent

2015 scenarios, by sector	Sector share	Growth rate Low Ebola	Growth rate High Ebola
Real GDP	*100.0*	*1.0*	*−5.2*
Agriculture	27.5	−0.3	−4.1
Forestry	7.2	0.7	−2.6
Mining and quarrying	13.9	10.3	−2.9
Manufacturing	4.7	−2.9	−6.9
Services	46.7	−0.9	−6.9

Source: World Bank estimates.

TABLE A.4
GDP Scenarios for Sierra Leone (2015)
Percent

2015 scenarios, by sector	Sector share	Growth rate Low Ebola	Growth rate High Ebola
Real GDP	*100.0*	*7.7*	*0.0*
Agriculture	27.5	2.4	−4.0
Forestry	7.2	2.3	0.5
Fisheries	5.5	2.0	1.4
Mining and quarrying	26.7	16.0	8.4
Other industry	4.0	9.7	2.0
Services	28.9	7.4	−4.4

Source: World Bank estimates.

Estimating the Expected Economic Impact across West Africa

As described in the text, our method for modeling the economic impact of the Ebola epidemic is to shock each of two computable general equilibrium (CGE) models with direct costs of illness (health-care spending), indirect costs of illness (the lost productivity of the dead and, during their illness, of the sick and their caregivers), and both the domestic and international aversion costs. We posit that, at least during 2014, aversion behavior due to fear of Ebola will generate economic losses that far exceed the direct and indirect costs of Ebola.

That the direct and indirect costs will be relatively small in 2014, and possibly also in 2015 can be inferred from a comparison of the estimated number of 2014 Ebola deaths with the pre-Ebola estimates of deaths from all other causes in Liberia, Sierra Leone, and Guinea in 2010. At this writing, the number of suspected or confirmed deaths from Ebola in Liberia, Sierra Leone, and Guinea in 2014 is more than 5,000.

Figure B.1 shows the distribution by cause of the approximately 200,000 deaths estimated to have occurred in Guinea (102,301), Sierra Leone (53,767), and Liberia (43,052) in 2010.[19] If the Ebola epidemic were to be arrested today in these three countries, Ebola would only slightly expand the category of "other communicable diseases." We would not be talking seriously about the economic impact of this disease.

But all of the causes of death catalogued in figure B.1 are endemic to these countries, varying little in their burden from year to year. Both business and labor have become somewhat accustomed to these health risks, and the recent rapid economic growth in all three of these countries has occurred despite this continuing disease burden.

Ebola is different. The number of Ebola cases and deaths, rather than remaining roughly constant from year-to-year, is growing at an increasing rate. When releasing its "roadmap" for intervention, the

FIGURE B.1
Estimated Annual Deaths in 2010 in Guinea, Sierra Leone, and Liberia, by Country and Cause of Death

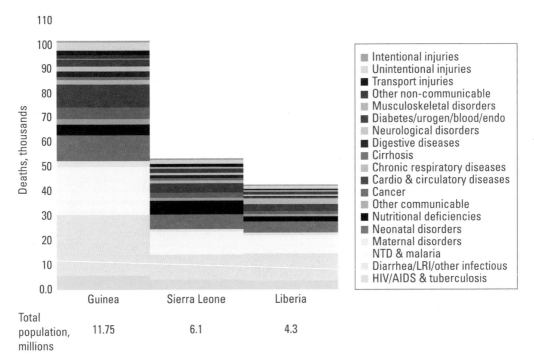

Source: Institute for Health Metrics and Evaluation 2014.
Note: HIV/AIDS = human immunodeficiency virus/acquired immune deficiency syndrome; LRI = lower respiratory infections; NTD = neglected tropical diseases.

WHO mentioned that the total number of cases for the whole duration of the outbreak might be held to 20,000 (WHO 2014b). At a 50 percent mortality rate, this estimate implies a total of about 10,000 deaths in Liberia, Sierra Leone, and Guinea. If the Ebola epidemic kills 10,000 people before it is controlled, which seems optimistic, it will rival HIV in its one-year impact on the disease burden in these three countries. This is the number of deaths to which we calibrate our "Low Ebola" estimates of economic impact.

More recent estimates from the CDC (Meltzer et al. 2014) and WHO (WHO Ebola Response Team 2014) give more pessimistic projections, with the former extrapolating to a total of 1.4 million cases or 700,000 deaths before the end of January 2015 in Liberia and Sierra Leone and the latter predicting 20,000 cases by early November, without adjusting for underreporting. If Ebola kills 700,000 before January 2015 and continues to grow thereafter, it would be killing more residents of these countries each year than would normally die in three or more years, a catastrophic mortality event that has not been seen on earth since the 1918 influenza epidemic.

Most observers believe that the Ebola epidemic will not continue to expand as fast as predicted by Meltzer et al. (2014). We have adopted a more moderate assumption for our High Ebola scenario: A total of 200,000 cases and about 100,000 deaths through 2015, with the Ebola outbreak extinguished before the end of 2015. Even worse scenarios are of course possible, but require extremely pessimistic assumptions regarding the scale-up of international assistance and the adaptive behavior of the affected populations.

The microeconomic and macroeconomic data cited in the text provide evidence that, despite the fact that the number of Ebola deaths that have so far occurred in Liberia, Sierra Leone, and Guinea is only a small fraction of annual deaths from other causes, the economic impact is already substantial. We ascribe this impact to both domestic and international aversion behavior. To capture this behavior in CGE models, we assume that aversion behavior can be translated into increased transaction costs and withdrawal from the production process of factors of production.

We distinguish transaction costs and factors of production by whether we deem them more likely to be affected by domestic or international aversion behavior. Domestic aversion behavior can be translated into a lockout or voluntary withdrawal of workers from places of employment and an increase in the cost associated with all domestic transactions, especially domestic transport. International aversion behavior can be translated into a reduction in the price received for exports combined with an increased cost of imports. Since a large share of the capital in the nascent manufacturing sectors of Liberia, Sierra Leone, and Guinea is foreign owned, we further assume that international aversion behavior will dramatically reduce FDI and also reduce the capacity utilization of existing capital stock.

All Ebola-related effects are expressed as percentages of baseline projections in the absence of the Ebola epidemic. We first establish these percentage shocks to transactions costs, prices, and factor supplies, which are sufficient for the MAMS CGE model of Liberia to generate the reductions in output growth that we anticipate in that country based on the sector decomposition methods described in the text and in appendix A. We then scale these shocks from a benchmark value of 100 in Liberia to reduced values in all other countries of the world.[20] To assign values, we construct an index scaling function based on two attributes of each country: the size of its potential Ebola outbreak and the strength and resilience of its health system and government. Specifically, we compute the index according to the following equation:

$$I_i = 100 \times \frac{P_i \times N_i}{Y^{1/2}} \times \frac{1}{L_i}$$

where i indexes the scenario, with $i = 1$ for the Low Ebola scenario and $i = 2$ for the High Ebola scenario. The variables are defined as follows:

I_i = index value for a given country, other than Liberia, for Ebola scenario i

P_i = probability of a single undetected seed case in any given month that the epidemic is active, for Ebola scenario i

N_i = number of cases within a month after the seed, given a single undetected seed case, for Ebola scenario i

Y = gross national product, which we assume to be correlated with the country's resilience and the strength of its health system.

$L_i = \dfrac{P_i \times N_i}{Y^{1/2}}$ for Liberia, for Ebola scenario i

We take the values of P_i and N_i from the results of a simulation model by Gomes et al. (2014). In this article, the authors embed a standard epidemiological model of Ebola transmission within a detailed model of the world transportation system to simulate the seeding of Ebola from one of the three most affected countries to other countries via air travel.

FIGURE B.2
Air Traffic Connections from West African Countries to the Rest of the World

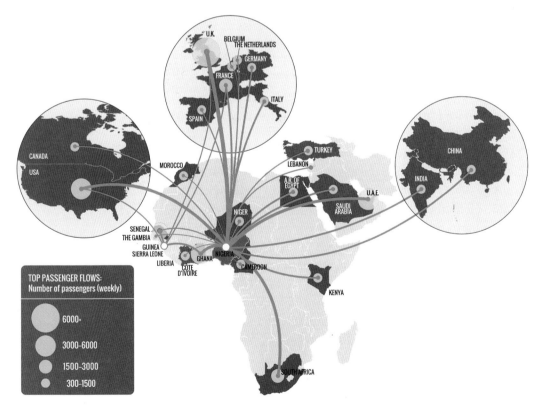

Source: Figure 1 of Gomes et al. (2014). Used with permission.

Figure B.2 displays a stylized map showing the number of passengers who travel on some of the most highly traveled air routes.

Of course, air travel is not the only or necessarily the principal form of disease spread. However, the Gomes et al. (2014) estimates represent the most systematic projections of disease spread to date. Gomes et al. simulate a month of the Ebola epidemic 10,000 times. Figure B.3, also reproduced from that article, displays the distribution of the number of Ebola cases that would appear in each of the 16 most frequently seeded countries. A large portion of the probability density is massed close to zero in each of the density plots, suggesting that no country has a high likelihood of being seeded. For the value of N_i in our index, we used either the 25th percentile number of cases (for the Low Ebola scenario) or the 99th percentile number of cases (for the High Ebola scenario).

FIGURE B.3
Frequency Distribution of Number of Cases of Ebola within One Month of the First Seeded Case

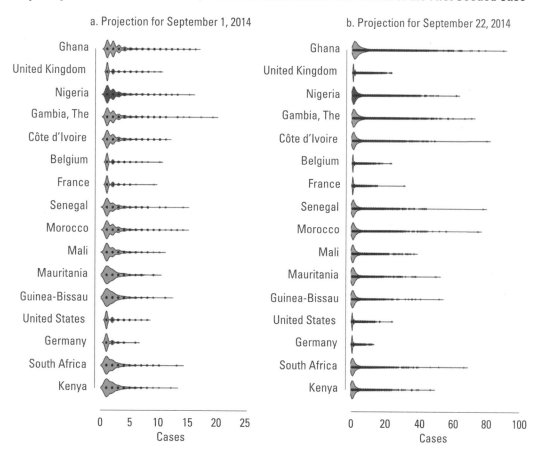

Source: Figure 4 of Gomes et al. (2014). Replicated with permission.

TABLE B.1
Ebola Impact Index

Country	Low Ebola					High Ebola			
	Probability of a seeded case in next 30 days	Number of cases if seeded in next 30 days	GDP (billions of 2013 US dollars)	Raw index	Scaled index	Probability of a seeded case in next 30 days	Number of cases if seeded in next 30 days	Raw index	Scaled index
Gambia, The	0.08	2	0.9	0.169	0.298	0.38	40	16.022	1.888
Guinea-Bissau	0.02	1	0.9	0.021	0.037	0.03	25	0.791	0.093
Liberia	*0.40*	*2*	*2.0*	*0.566*	*1.000*	*0.60*	*20*	*8.485*	*1.000*
Mauritania	0.02	1	4.2	0.010	0.017	0.03	18	0.263	0.031
Sierra Leone	0.40	2	4.9	0.361	0.639	0.60	20	5.421	0.639
Guinea	0.40	2	6.2	0.321	0.568	0.60	20	4.819	0.568
Mali	0.03	2	10.9	0.018	0.032	0.04	19	0.230	0.027
Senegal	0.03	1	15.1	0.008	0.014	0.09	49	1.135	0.134
Côte d'Ivoire	0.06	2	30.9	0.022	0.038	0.14	44	1.108	0.131
Kenya	0.01	1	44.1	0.002	0.003	0.05	8	0.060	0.007
Ghana	0.35	2	47.9	0.101	0.179	0.57	53	4.365	0.514
Morocco	0.03	2	104.4	0.006	0.010	0.15	41	0.602	0.071
South Africa	0.01	2	350.6	0.001	0.002	0.09	46	0.221	0.026
Belgium	0.05	1	508.1	0.002	0.004	0.10	13	0.058	0.007
Nigeria	0.11	2	522.6	0.010	0.017	0.18	52	0.409	0.048
United Kingdom	0.25	1	2,522.3	0.005	0.009	0.29	17	0.098	0.012
France	0.03	1	2,734.9	0.001	0.001	0.06	33	0.038	0.004
Germany	0.01	1	3,634.8	0.000	0.0003	0.04	20	0.013	0.002
United States	0.01	1	16,800.0	0.000	0.0001	0.15	18	0.021	0.002

Note: Raw index is the product of the probability of a seeded case and the number of cases if seeded. The scaled index is the raw index divided by GDP$^{1/2}$, which proxies for the quality of the health system (to be able to contain the spread of cases), but with diminishing marginal returns. All country impacts are scaled down from estimates for Liberia.

FIGURE B.4
Scatter Plot of the Ebola Impact Index against a Country's GDP for the Low Ebola Scenario

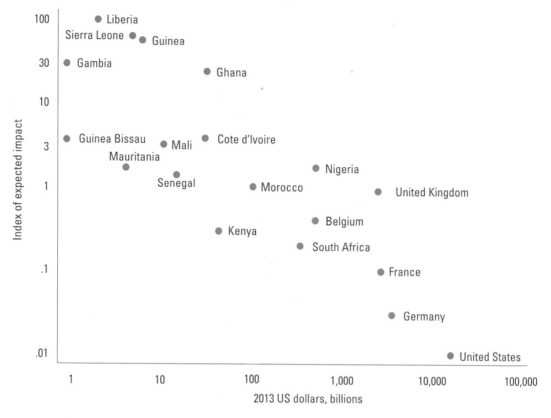

Source: World Bank calculations.

Using these values for P_i and N_i, we construct index values for all
the countries in the LINKAGE model. Figure B.4 displays a scatter plot
of our index against a country's GDP. Note that countries with higher
GDPs, by our assumption, are much less vulnerable when a single case
is seeded. At any given GDP, a country has a higher index if it has
either a higher probability of being seeded or a higher number of cases
if seeded. The probabilities, numbers of cases, and index factors are
listed in table B.1.

The countries with the highest impact index in figure B.4 will not
necessarily be seeded with a case of Ebola, nor will they necessarily
greatly suffer if they are. However, the Ebola impact index does
suggest which countries are in greatest danger of potential infection.
As long as the Ebola epidemic is present among some West African
populations, each week constitutes a new "throw of the dice," which
could lead to the arrival of a new Ebola-infected individual in any of
the above countries.

The LINKAGE model uses these Ebola Impact Index values to scale down the perturbations that we assume are introduced because of aversion behavior. By virtue of both their GDP and their relatively few links by air with Liberia, Sierra Leone, and Guinea, the U.S. and Germany are not predicted to bear a large Ebola burden. But all the West African countries are at risk to one or another degree.

Modeling the Economic
Impact on West Africa

Introduction

The medium-term estimates of the economic implications of the Ebola outbreak in West Africa are based on simulations using the World Bank's dynamic computable general equilibrium (CGE) model called LINKAGE. A CGE model uses economic data and a set of behavioral equations to estimate how an economy might react to changes in policy, technology, or other factors. The model is benchmarked to a starting year dataset that covers the whole economy, tracking the inter-linkages between sectors through input-output or inter-industry transaction flow tables, various sources of demand such as intermediate demand of enterprises and final demand of households, government, and investment. It also models the behavior of producers through profit-maximizing production functions. Finally, it simulates foreign demand and supply by including equations explaining bilateral trade flows.

The analysis using a CGE model starts from the development of a baseline with a set of exogenous variables and parameters (population, productivity growth, and elasticities). Then the counterfactual policy scenario is formulated by changing some exogenous variables or policy parameters. Finally, the impact of a counterfactual scenario is assessed by looking at deviations of endogenous variables (i.e., those variables that are not fixed or user-specified) from their baseline levels (e.g., GDP, investment, savings, trade flows, sectoral output, employment, wages, household consumption, welfare, and relative prices).

CGE models are best thought of as tools used for understanding the implications of different scenarios. Thanks to their rich structure, they capture complex inter-linkages between sectors and countries.

However, they cannot track the short-term dynamics of an economy; and by focusing only on the developments in the real sphere of the economy, they cannot be used as forecasting tools. The CGE models cannot be tested for statistical accuracy of a forecast in the same way that econometric models can be. In short, these are tools for scenario analysis, not for forecasting.

Methodology

This section covers the main features of LINKAGE, while a full description is provided in technical papers by van der Mensbrugghe (2011) and van der Mensbrugghe (2013). The current version of LINKAGE largely relies on release 8.1 of the GTAP database (Global Trade Analysis Program 2014). The data include social accounting matrices and bilateral trade flows for 134 countries/regions and 57 sectors. For computational and analytical purposes, the version employed in this study includes 12 countries/regions and 6 sectors. For the detailed regions, see table C.1 below. The database is benchmarked to 2007; we update it to 2013 replicating the key macroeconomic aggregates (GDP growth, investment, and current account).

The core specification of the model replicates a largely standard global CGE model.[21] Production is specified as a series of nested constant elasticity of substitution (CES) functions for the various inputs—unskilled and skilled labor, capital, land, natural resources (sector-specific), energy, and other material inputs. The structure of the CES nest characterizes the substitution and complementary relations across inputs. LINKAGE uses a vintage structure of production that allows for putty-semi-putty capital. This means that capital can be either old or new, with new capital being more substitutable with other factors. This implies that countries with relatively high rates of investment, such as China, will tend to have more flexible economies as their share of new capital tends to be higher than in countries with relatively low rates of investment. In the labor market in the baseline, we assume full employment and allow for internal migration even though there is no international migration. Aggregate land supply follows a logistic curve with an absolute maximum available supply calibrated to International Institute for Applied Systems Analysis data.

The assumptions on productivity growth are complex. Different approaches are adapted to three broad sectors: agriculture, manufacturing, and services. Agricultural productivity is assumed to be factor-neutral and exogenous and is set to estimates from empirical studies (Martin and Mitra 2001). Productivity in manufacturing and services is labor-augmenting and skill-neutral but sector-biased. The productivity

TABLE C.1
Region and Sector Compositions in LINKAGE Model

Regions	Rest of Western Africa
High-income countries	Benin
United States	Burkina Faso
EU27 and EFTA	Cabo Verde
China	Cameroon
India	Côte d'Ivoire
Less developed countries	Gambia, The
Ghana	Guinea
Nigeria	Guinea-Bissau
Senegal	Liberia
Rest of Western Africa	Mali
South Africa	Mauritania
Rest of Africa	Niger
	Sierra Leone
	Togo
Sectors	
Agriculture	
Natural resources	
Trade	
Manufacturing	
Transport	
Services	

Source: World Bank.
Note: EFTA = European Free Trade Association; EU = European Union.

growth assumptions in manufacturing and services are country-specific and based on past trends in productivity growth. Following the broad findings of earlier researchers (Bosworth and Collins 2007), we assume that productivity growth in manufacturing is about 2 percentage points faster than in services.

Demand by each domestic agent is specified at the so-called Armington level, that is demand for a bundle of domestically produced and imported goods. Armington demand is aggregated across all agents and allocated at the national level between domestic production and imports by region of origin. A top level CES nest first allocates aggregate (or Armington) demand between domestic production and an aggregate import bundle. A second-level nest then allocates aggregate imports across the model's different regions, thus generating a bilateral trade flow matrix. Each bilateral flow is associated with three price wedges. The first distinguishes producer prices from the FOB (free-on-board) price (an export tax and/or subsidy). The second distinguishes the FOB price from the CIF (cost, insurance, and freight) price (an international trade and transportation margin). The third distinguishes the CIF price from the user price (an import tariff).

Governments derive their income from various taxes: sales, excise duties, import duties, exports, production, factors, and direct taxes. Investment revenues come from household, government, and net foreign savings. Government and investment expenditure are based on CES functions.

The standard scenario incorporates three closure rules. Typically government expenditures are held constant as a share of GDP; fiscal balance is exogenous, while direct taxes adjust to cover any changes in the revenues to keep the fiscal balance at the exogenous level. The second closure rule determines the investment savings balance. Households save a portion of their income with the average propensity to save influenced by demographics and economic growth. Government savings and foreign savings are exogenous in the current specification. As a result, investment is savings driven and the total amount of savings depends on household savings, with the price of investment goods being determined also by demand for investment. The last closure determines the external balance. In the current application, we fix the foreign savings and therefore the trade balance. Therefore, changes in trade flows will result in shifts in the real exchange rate.

The model characterizes a few key dynamics. Population growth is based on the medium fertility variant of the United Nations' population projections. Labor force growth is equated to the growth of the working age population—defined here as the demographic cohort between 15 and 64 years of age. Investment is equated to total savings. Household savings are a function of income growth and demographic dependency ratios, with savings rising as incomes rise and dependency ratios decline. Thus, countries that have declining youth dependency rates tend to see a rise in savings. This will eventually be offset by countries that have a rising share of elderly in their population, which will result in a fall in savings. Capital accumulation is then equated to the previous period's (depreciated) capital stock plus investment. Productivity growth in the baseline is "calibrated" to achieve the growth rates for the baseline scenario as in the IMF World Economic Outlook database for 2014 and 2015. These productivity growth rates remain fixed in the counterfactual scenarios.

Capturing the Economic Impact of Ebola

We develop three scenarios. The baseline (no Ebola) replicates the World Bank/IMF forecast for 2014 and 2015 constructed before the emergence of Ebola. We replicate the GDP, investment, and current account numbers for these years. To study the impact of Ebola, we analyze two scenarios: Low Ebola and High Ebola. These are based on the probabilities of international spread of Ebola from Gomes et al. (2014) with lower probabilities defining Low Ebola and higher probabilities defining High Ebola: These two scenarios are described in detail in appendix B. In both scenarios, the outbreak of Ebola spreads to some extent to other countries in West Africa, while in High Ebola the outbreak also spreads to other African countries.

The impact of Ebola has been translated through two channels. The first channel is through a reduction in factors of production: lower labor supply growth rates and capital underutilization. The first, direct effects on the labor force consist of workers being ill, dying, or caring for the ill. While tragic, this amounts to a relatively small proportion of the labor force. The much larger shock comes from workers staying at home for fear of exposure to Ebola or because businesses reduce capacity and force workers to take unpaid leave. At the same time, capital remains underutilized. This is similarly due to closures or reductions in the operational capacity of factories and businesses. The decline in factor availability reduces the productive capacity of the economy and results in reductions in output and household income.

The second channel is through increased transport and transaction costs in domestic and foreign trade. Increased domestic and international trade and transaction margins arise due to inspections, market and road closures, border closures, and so on. These will lower the prices that domestic producers receive for their products and services net of transaction costs, and will increase the prices of imports on the domestic market. Increased domestic transaction costs in domestic trade lead to efficiency losses and reduce the income of domestic producers. These two channels combined account for the full impact of Ebola (see figure C.1), and are likely to result in lower trade, investment, output, household income, and consumption, as well as worsening of terms of trade, all of which are endogenous in the simulations.

FIGURE C.1
How the LINKAGE Model Works

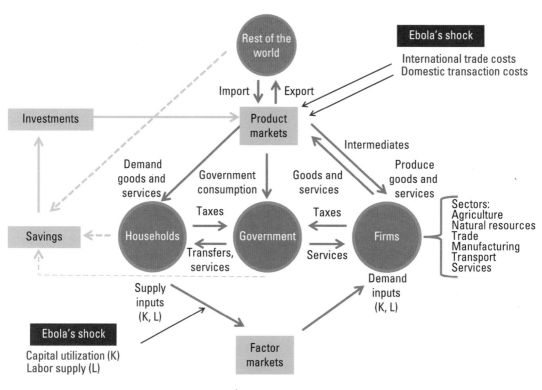

Source: World Bank.

The assumptions regarding reductions in factors of production and international and domestic transaction costs for the West Africa region are presented in table C.2. All of these effects are then scaled according to the probability of having a case and the likely number of cases, as explained in appendix B. In the Low Ebola case, labor force growth drops from 2.3 percent to 2.1 percent in 2014 due to mortality and morbidity (a small fraction), and aversion behavior—individuals avoiding markets or traveling across borders. The shock resulting from aversion behavior is moderate because labor force growth is assumed to have been normal for the first nine months of 2014. In 2015, the growth rate returns to normal (from a smaller base due to the shock in 2014). In the High Ebola case, the shock is more pronounced due to a more rapid spread of the outbreak to other countries in the region, and it continues into 2015. Capital utilization follows a similar pattern in both scenarios. Finally, aversion behavior, as well as additional costs due to inspections, border closures, and so forth, are captured by increases in the "trade and transaction margins," with a moderate shock in the second half of 2014 but then a return to normal in 2015 in the Low Ebola case. In the High Ebola case, the shock is more pronounced in 2014 and then continues into the first half of 2015.

We report the results of the simulations for West Africa as a whole (see table C.3). In the baseline, the GDP of West Africa would have been expected to grow by 6.7 percent in 2014 and by 6.4 percent in 2015.

TABLE C.2
Assumptions about Changes in Factor Availability in the West Africa Region as Compared with the Baseline (2014–15)
Percent

	Baseline		Low Ebola		High Ebola	
Variables	2014	2015	2014	2015	2014	2015
Labor force growth rates	2.3	2.3	2.2	2.3	1.7	0.9
Capital utilization	100	100	99.2	99.9	97.7	95.6
Trade and transaction margins[a]	100	100	102	100	105	110

Source: World Bank projections based on LINKAGE model.
a. International trade and domestic transaction margins. The increase of trade and transaction margins shown above refers to the Rest of West Africa regional aggregate, while the impacts are scaled for Ghana, Senegal, and Nigeria, as well as other regions.

TABLE C.3
Annual GDP Growth Rates of the West Africa Region in the Baseline and the Low Ebola and High Ebola Scenarios (2013–15)
Percent

	(1)	(2)	(3)	(4)	(5)	(6)	(7)
		Baseline		Low Ebola		High Ebola	
Variables	2013	2014	2015	2014	2015	2014	2015
Investment	100	107.7	117.5	107.6	120.6	104.4	106.3
Price of exports[a]	100	100	100	98.5	100	96.4	93.3
Exports	100	109.6	119.3	107.6	119.2	104.0	105.7
GDP volume	100	106.7	113.5	106.4	113.3	105.6	109.9
GDP annual growth rates	6.9	6.7	6.4	6.4	6.5	5.6	4.1
GDP (2013 USD billion)	709.3	756.6	805.2	754.4	803.5	749.3	779.9
GDP lost (USD billion)	—	—	—	2.2	1.6	7.35	25.2

Source: World Bank projections based on LINKAGE model.
Note: Dollar figures are in 2013 US dollars.
a. Price of exports net of transaction costs.

Furthermore, transaction costs remain at the 2013 level and exports were projected to increase by 7.7 percent in 2014 and by 9 percent in 2015.

In Low Ebola, when the outbreak is contained relatively quickly, the impact on the economy is quite limited (see table C.3). The growth rate in 2014 slows down by 0.3 percentage points, but it recovers in 2015 when Ebola is under control for most of the year. With lower income, household savings decline and there is less funding for investment. Indeed, investment declines by 0.1 percentage points relative to the baseline value for 2014. Producers lose part of the value of their products due to increased trade and transport margins, which—coupled with lower output—lead to a reduction in the volume of exports relative to the baseline by 2 percentage points (see table C.3, columns 2 and 4). The forgone output due to lower GDP growth is worth approximately US$2.2 billion in 2013 dollars (see last row of table C.3).[22] When output recovers in the second half of 2015 and transaction costs return to the baseline level, exports expand to reach a volume similar to the baseline level, but GDP is now increasing from a lower base (due to a drop in 2014),[23] and the output volume in 2015 in the Low Ebola scenario is still US$1.6 billion below the baseline level (see figure C.2).[24]

With a large expansion of the outbreak and Ebola spreading to other countries within the region (accounting for 83 percent of West Africa's

FIGURE C.2
GDP Volume and Growth Rates in the Baseline and Low Ebola and High Ebola Scenarios (2013–15)

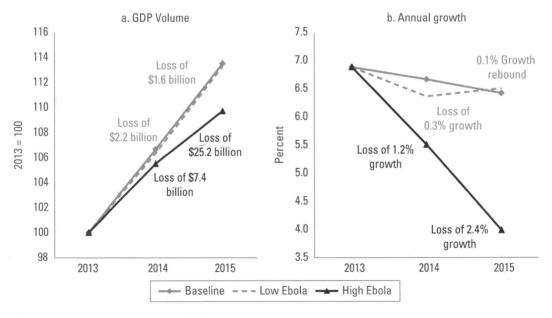

Source: World Bank calculations using LINKAGE.

GDP in 2013), there is a more significant reduction in labor and utilization of capital. In addition, transaction costs increase by a further 3 percentage points, and the impact on exports and imports is much more significant. Export growth would be over 5 percentage points lower in 2014 in the High Ebola scenario compared to the baseline. Exports recover in 2015, but their volume remains significantly below their baseline value in 2014. The GDP growth rate declines to 4.1 percent in 2014. This is the value of GDP growth for the West Africa region as a whole, which indicates that for the countries directly affected by the Ebola outbreak the economic decline is likely to be much more significant. Building on the assumptions in Gomes et al. (2014), we model the six countries or country groupings[25] most likely to have an Ebola outbreak, assuming the disease does not travel beyond those.

The resulting slower growth rate leads to in a reduction in output worth US$7.35 in 2014. Output continues to grow at a much slower rate in 2015 than in the baseline case, leading to a further loss of US$25.2 billion.[26] Overall, in the High Ebola scenario, West Africa's GDP is only 10 percent higher than its 2013 level by the end of 2015, while in the absence of Ebola it would have been 19 percent higher (see table C.3, columns 3 and 7). In addition to the immeasurable costs of lives lost, the loss of income under High Ebola could take years to recover.

With swift international action, Ebola can be contained, thousands of precious lives could be saved, and the economic cost for the region could be limited. If the outbreak is not contained, the economic costs could run into billions of U.S. dollars in forgone output (up to $33 billion). Our results indicate that acting fast saves precious lives and that spending even billions of dollars to contain the spread would be cost-effective.

In the High Ebola scenario, the rest of Africa is also negatively affected. Even though the spread of Ebola to other countries beyond West Africa is very small, there is already a noticeable economic impact on other African economies, mainly due to higher trade and transaction costs. For example, we estimate that the impact on South Africa would be to reduce its GDP level in 2015 by 0.3 percentage points relative to the baseline 2015 level (see figure C.3). South Africa is one of the top five trading partners for Nigeria (exports) and Sierra Leone (imports), so even without being directly affected by Ebola it is likely to experience a lower GDP growth. This impact is likely to be significantly bigger once we incorporate the impact of the fear factor and the diversion of tourism, investment, and trade from other African countries.

As already stated in the introduction, these scenarios should not be perceived as forecasts. The CGE simulations simply allow us to analyze various scenarios in a consistent and coherent framework.

FIGURE C.3
Forgone GDP in West Africa (High Ebola—2015)

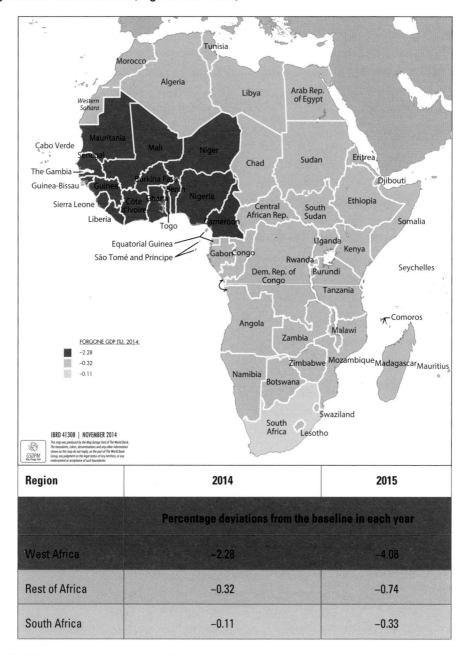

Region	2014	2015
	Percentage deviations from the baseline in each year	
West Africa	−2.28	−4.08
Rest of Africa	−0.32	−0.74
South Africa	−0.11	−0.33

Source: World Bank estimation based on LINKAGE's CGE model.

Our estimates may even be underestimated because the most recent epidemiological projections indicate that in the worst-case scenario, the number of cases could reach over one million, and how aversion behavior varies with caseload is not known with precision. This analysis also does not incorporate every possible economic implication of the epidemic. Further, if the fear factor persists and reduces investment and trade for years to come, the negative growth implications could continue well beyond 2015.

Modeling the Economic Impact on Liberia

This appendix offers a rapid assessment of the possible impact on Liberia's economy of Ebola based on simulations with MAMS, a Computable General Equilibrium (CGE) model developed by the World Bank for analysis of the impact of policy changes and economic shocks in developing countries.[27] The simulations, which are based on a detailed Liberian database, address two alternative Ebola scenarios: A moderate case underpinned by effective policies leading to rapid containment (Low Ebola) and a severe case with an inadequate policy response leading to slow containment (High Ebola). As noted in the main body of the text, in broad outline, the results and the assumptions are similar but not identical to those of the sector decomposition analysis; this is due to differences in detailed assumptions and method.

The advantage of a model of this type is that it imposes basic economic mechanisms, including markets with flexible prices and the constraints and linkages that are important in any economy: Employment of labor, capital, and other factors is limited to what is available; production in one sector generates demands for the outputs of downstream sectors and meets the demands of upstream sectors, households, investors, and exporters; private and government incomes from production, transfers (including grant aid and private remittances), and other sources (for the government including taxes) generate demands for domestic output and imports; and the spending of the nation as a whole and for each type of agent (the government, firms and households) must be fully financed (by some combination of current incomes, grants, and net borrowing, some of which may come from abroad).

In this application, the results for alternative Ebola scenarios in 2014 and 2015 are compared to a baseline scenario that reflects the expected development of Liberia's economy before the emergence of Ebola.

This comparison assesses the effects of Ebola on country-level macro, sectoral, welfare, and poverty indicators. In sum, a comparison between two possible Ebola scenarios, representing success and failure to contain the epidemic, demonstrate the dramatic importance of making sure that workers can access their places of work and that trade can continue without interruptions and excessive transaction costs. This requires that the epidemic be stopped in the very near future.

Scenario Assumptions

- The analysis looks at the impact of two Ebola scenarios, contrasting them with a baseline scenario without Ebola.

- The first Ebola scenario, labeled Low Ebola, assumes that an effective policy response is rapidly implemented by the end of 2014, putting an end to new cases and deaths. As a result, the economic repercussions are kept in check.

- The second Ebola scenario, High Ebola, assumes that the policy response is slow and ineffective, leading to a much larger number of cases and deaths in 2014 as well as additional deaths in 2015 before the virus is contained and defeated. Accordingly, the economic repercussions are much more severe.

- Table D.1 summarizes the key assumptions for the two scenarios. The assumptions are based on the fragmentary evidence available at the time of writing this report. In addition to losses in life, such evidence indicates that Ebola makes itself felt through multiple economic channels, the most important of which are the following:

  o Labor. Due to fear, controls, and restrictions on movement, workers do not go to work, reducing the productive capacity of the economy.

  o Mining. Like other sectors, production in mining is reduced. The mining sector is singled out given its importance and the fact that its production and exports depend critically on the presence of expatriates, that is, not on the general reduction in the labor supply in the economy.

  o FDI declines because of added uncertainty about the future and interruptions to international travel and communication.

  o Trade (or transactions) costs increase. Such costs arise when goods are brought from the border to domestic demanders (for imports)

and from domestic suppliers to the border or to domestic demanders (for exports and sales of domestic output domestically, respectively). These costs increase due to the same forces that keep
workers away from their workplaces. In the context of the simulations, they require labor and other inputs and contribute to relatively strong growth for private services. They represent a
productivity loss since additional inputs are needed to bring goods
to their demanders inside or outside of Liberia's economy, instead
of being available for consumption and investment. For the agricultural sectors, these effects are milder since a substantial part of production is consumed by the producers themselves or in the local
community, mitigating the impact of higher trade costs.

o Foreign grants. The international community is increasing its aid,
especially for health spending to contain Ebola.

TABLE D.1
Key Assumptions for MAMS Liberia Simulations (2014–15)

	Low Ebola[a]		High Ebola[a]	
	2014[b]	2015[b]	2014[b]	2015[b]
Ebola cases	12,000	0	120,000	30,000
Ebola deaths[c]	6,900	0	69,000	17,000
Labor employment (% decline from baseline in same year)[d]	2.9	0.5	11.3	14.1
Mining resource use (% decline from baseline in same year)	5.7	0.4	16.3	19.1
Foreign direct investment (% decline from baseline in same year)	−41.5	−14.7	−41.5	−57.3
Additional export and import trade costs (% of border price)[e]	15.0	0.0	22.5	22.5
Additional domestic trade costs (% of producer price)	17.5	0.0	26.3	26.3
Additional foreign grants (million 2014 US dollars)	47.7	95.4	15.7	31.5

Note: MAMS = Maquette for Millennium Development Goal Simulations.
a. Low Ebola and High Ebola reflect moderate (strong policy) and severe (weak policy) impact scenarios, respectively.
b. The years are calendar years.
c. The majority (in all the simulations) of the deaths afflict persons in working age (15–64 years old).
d. This decline in labor force is due to fear and movement restrictions and is in addition to the loss due to death. In the
model, the decline is imposed via a lower labor force participation rate among the population aged 15–64 years.
e. These trade costs reflect use of services to bring goods from the supplier to the border (for exports) and from the border
to the domestic demander (for imports). For exports, the added trade costs reduce the price of the producer relative to the
border price; for imports, it adds to the price paid by demanders relative to the border price. These cost additions are at
base prices; they may be smaller or larger depending on changes in the prices of trade services.

Simulation Results

Low Ebola

The growth rates under Low Ebola are compared to the baseline scenario
in figure D.1. In 2014, the impact on several variables is moderate, in part
due to the fact that the crisis emerged during the second half of the year.
For the government—here broadly defined to include the government-
type activities of non-government organizations and other donors—the
effects are relatively mild since foreign grants, its major revenue source,
increase at the same time as the decline in the economic activities that
generate tax revenues is moderate. It is assumed that the government
maintains its domestic borrowing unchanged in real terms (i.e., compared
to the baseline increasing as a share of GDP due to a lower GDP level). In
response to the health crisis, the government reallocates spending, compared to the baseline, significantly raising its consumption and reducing

FIGURE D.1
Macroeconomic Growth in Liberia under Low Ebola (2014–15)

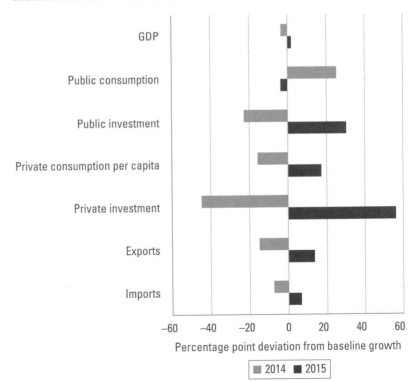

Source: World Bank calculations.

its investment. As a result of the decline in the employment of labor, the model predicts a decline in household incomes, savings, and consumption. Coupled with the decline in FDI, lower household savings translate into less financing of private investment.

The increase in transaction costs also raises the prices households pay for their consumption items. The fact that a substantial part of domestic consumption of agricultural goods is represented by consumption by farm households from their own production or the production of the local community mitigates the impact of transaction costs on average food prices from domestic sources. Higher transaction costs also discourage exports and imports, even though the effects under this scenario are quite small. In figure D.1, household consumption is measured in per capita terms to correct for the fact that the population is slightly smaller than under the baseline scenario. The fact that Liberia suffers from a demographic dividend in reverse (its dependency ratio increases due to Ebola deaths) and a larger share of its working age population is inactive exacerbates the decline in consumption per capita.

This scenario posits that in 2015, thanks to a successful health intervention, few or no additional Ebola cases or deaths are recorded, and the negative economic shocks of 2014 are mostly reversed; most importantly, lifting restrictions on people's movements makes it possible to allocate most labor back to production while trade costs return to normal levels. Moreover, the emergency response is pulled back, reducing public consumption and raising public investment, bringing the economy toward its original trajectory. Still, due to the need for some time to restart the economy, including time lags in production processes in agriculture and elsewhere, lingering uncertainties (affecting mining and FDI), and less investment in 2014, GDP is still below the baseline level in 2015. The net impacts of these developments on the growth rates of macro indicators are shown in figure D.1: Most important, the changes in public and private investment and household consumption are reversed, while public consumption, supported by continued aid, remains above the baseline 2015 level even though its growth has slowed. The impact on households is reflected in figure D.2, which shows the headcount poverty rate under different scenarios: For Low Ebola, the 2015 poverty rate returns to close to the (still substantial) baseline rate for the year.[28]

Figure D.3 shows how growth in sector value-added under Low Ebola deviates from the baseline scenario. In 2014, the economy shifted temporarily toward higher public and private service production at the expense of agriculture and industry, including mining. In 2015, the opposite happened, bringing the economy closer to initial shares.

FIGURE D.2
Headcount Poverty Rate under Alternative Scenarios (2013–15)

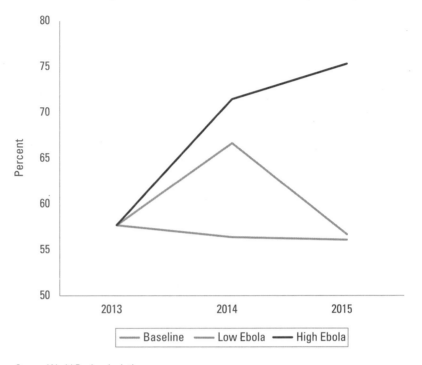

Source: World Bank calculations.

FIGURE D.3
Sector-Specific Growth under Low Ebola (2014–15)

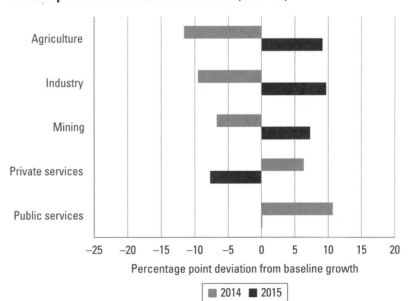

Source: World Bank calculations.

High Ebola

Compared to the Low Ebola scenario, the High Ebola scenario demonstrates that, in the absence of a concerted policy response, a much more
severe calamity may afflict Liberia and other countries in its neighborhood
and beyond. Under this scenario, as the number of cases and deaths spirals
out of control in the last few months of 2014, the economy is near collapse,
with large-scale withdrawal of labor from production and more severe
increases in trade costs, accompanied by very limited aid increases (see
table D.1). Figure D.4 summarizes the macro consequences. In 2014, due
to access to fewer resources, the public investment cut is more dramatic.
Household income losses are larger and their purchasing power suffers
from the additional increase in trade costs, translating into more dramatic
cuts in savings, private investment, and household per capita consumption. Exports (for mining and other sectors) decline, together with the
decline in FDI and lower grant aid, adding to the need to cut imports.
Only public consumption growth increases compared to the baseline but is
below the level for the Low Ebola scenario.

FIGURE D.4
Macroeconomic Growth in Liberia under High Ebola (2014–15)

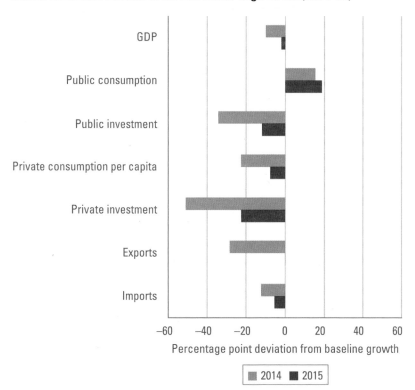

Source: World Bank calculations.

FIGURE D.5
Sector-Specific Growth Rates under High Ebola (2014–15)

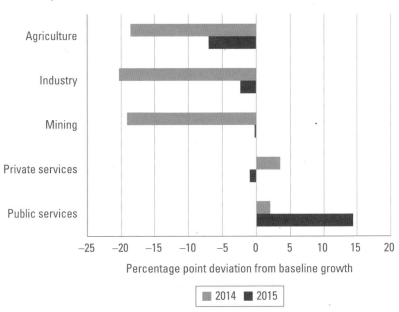

Source: World Bank calculations.

As a result of the failure to put an end to the epidemic during 2014, the crisis becomes more severe in 2015, with continued new Ebola cases and deaths, stronger negative shocks from additional withdrawal of labor from production, further cuts in FDI, continued high trade costs, and only a moderate increase in aid from the international community. The end result is continued growth below baseline scenario rates for GDP, private and public investment, private consumption, and imports. Exports return to the baseline growth rate (after the strong decline in 2014), whereas public consumption, thanks to the aid increase and public investment cut, grows faster than under the baseline (figure D.1). The continued decline in per capita household consumption dramatically raises the headcount poverty rate (figure D.2). Growth in sector value-added matches these developments (figure D.5): After the sharp decline in 2014, growth is negative or only moderately positive for all sectors except public services.

Notes

1. Hereafter, the term *Ebola* is used to refer to the virus, the disease, or the epidemic outbreak.
2. West Africa, in this analysis, includes Benin, Burkina Faso, Cabo Verde, Cameroon, Côte d'Ivoire, The Gambia, Ghana, Guinea, Guinea-Bissau, Liberia, Mali, Mauritania, Niger, Nigeria, Senegal, Sierra Leone, and Togo.
3. The U.S. Centers for Disease Control uses an underreporting factor of 2.5 (Meltzer et al. 2014).
4. For example, an annualized growth rate of 6 percent for the first half of the year, followed by an annualized rate of 0.6 percent in the second half—representing a 90 percent reduction in the original annual growth rate—would still yield an overall growth of 3.3 percent for the full year.
5. Construction is included under services in the Liberian presentation of the national accounts.
6. Specific objectives of the exercise were to (a) reach 1.5 million households across Sierra Leone with correct information about Ebola; (b) increase community acceptance of Ebola-affected persons, especially children; (c) promote hand washing with soap at the household level (1.5 million bars of soap will be distributed); (d) rebuild public confidence and trust in the health system; and (e) install neighborhood watch structures at the community level.
7. This method is described in detail in appendix A.
8. Background information on the MAMS application to Liberia is found in Lofgren (2013). Its application here is described in detail in appendix D. The model itself is fully documented in Lofgren, Cicowiez, and Diaz-Bonilla (2013).
9. This method is described in detail in appendix C.
10. The 12 region/country aggregates are high-income countries, United States, European Union-27 and European Free Trade Association, China, India, less-developed countries, Ghana, Nigeria, Senegal, Rest of Western Africa, South Africa, and Rest of Africa.
11. Grady reports projections of more than 50,000 cases just by October 12.
12. The report eschews analysis of low probability worst case scenarios, such as might occur if cases seed and spread undetected in most African urban centers. In the MAMS Liberia analysis, the High Ebola scenario is based on the more pessimistic (but not implausible) assumption that Ebola worsens significantly compared to the Low (or central) case already occurring in 2014.

13. The poverty data are generated assuming that inequality does not change—available data is not sufficient to determine the likely impact of Ebola on inequality.

14. The GDP is incorporated as a square root, which captures diminishing returns to income in terms of health-care system quality.

15. Even countries that have successfully combatted cases previously have the unfortunate potential for re-exposure as long as the Ebola epidemic is present among some West African populations.

16. These are Ghana, Nigeria, Senegal, South Africa, the rest of West Africa, and the rest of Africa. The rest of West Africa includes Benin, Burkina Faso, Cape Verde, the Gambia, Guinea, Guinea-Bissau, Liberia, Mali, Mauritania, Niger, Saint Helena, Ascension and Tristan Da Cunha, Sierra Leone and Togo. The rest of Africa includes Algeria, Angola, Botswana, Cameroon, Côte d'Ivoire, the Central African Republic, Chad, Congo, Democratic Republic of Congo, Egypt, Equatorial Guinea, Gabon, Kenya, Lesotho, Libya, Madagascar, Malawi, Mauritius, Morocco, Mozambique, Namibia, São Tomé and Principe, Swaziland, Tanzania, Tunisia, Uganda, Western Sahara, Zambia, and Zimbabwe.

17. These values (loss of US$7.35 billion in 2014 and US$25.2 billion in 2015) refer to the difference between the estimated GDP in the High Ebola scenario compared to the baseline scenario (no Ebola), for the respective years.

18. After the SARS and H1N1 epidemics and again in response to the avian flu, donors resolved to strengthen the epidemiological surveillance systems in poor countries by investing in primary care systems, referral networks, and diagnostic reporting. Sustained, effective efforts are required.

19. Lower and upper bounds for the three countries are 171,000–232,000. See Wang et al. (2012).

20. In the High Ebola scenario, the Gambia is the only instance of a country that has a larger expected index value than Liberia.

21. Other well-known models in this class include the GTAP model (Hertel 1998) and CEPII's Mirage (Decreux and Valin 2007).

22. This value refers to the difference between the estimated GDP in the baseline scenario (no Ebola) compared to the Low Ebola scenario.

23. This is the reason the GDP growth rate (in percentage points) in 2015 is higher in Low Ebola than in the baseline scenario (see "growth rebound" in figure C.2).

24. The level of GDP (volumes) in the Low Ebola scenario is lower than the baseline projection.

25. These are Ghana, Nigeria, Senegal, South Africa and the rest of Africa.

26. These values (loss of US$7.35 billion in 2014 and US$25.2 billion in 2015) refer to the difference between the estimated GDP in the High Ebola scenario compared to the baseline scenario (no Ebola), for the respective years.

27. Additional information is also found at www.worldbank.org/mams.

28. The poverty calculation assumes that inequality (measured by the Gini coefficient) does not change and that consumption follows a log-normal distribution.

References

Bosworth, Barry, and Susan M. Collins. 2007. "Accounting for Growth: Comparing China and India." NBER Working Paper 12943, National Bureau of Economic Research, Cambridge, MA.

Clarke, Toni, and Saliou Samb. 2014. "UN Says $600 Million Needed to Tackle Ebola as Deaths Top 1,900." *Reuters*, September 3.

Decreux, Yvan, and Hugo Valin. 2007. "MIRAGE, Updated Version of the Model for Trade Policy Analysis: Focus on Agriculture and Dynamics." CEPII Document de travail 15, CEPII, Paris.

FAO (Food and Agriculture Organization). 2014. *Food Security Brief: Ebola Virus Disease*. Washington, DC: FAO of the United Nations.

Global Trade Analysis Program. 2014. http://www.gtap.org. Purdue University, Lafayette, IN.

Gomes, Marcelo F. C., Ana Pastore y Piontti, Luca Rossi, Dennis Chao, Ira Longini, M. Elizabeth Halloran, and Alessandro Vespignani. 2014. "Assessing the International Spreading Risk Associated with the 2014 West African Ebola Outbreak." *PLOS Current Outbreaks*, September 2.

Grady, Denise. 2014. "U.S. Scientists See Long Fight against Ebola." *New York Times*, September 12.

Hertel, Thomas W. 1998. *Global Trade Analysis: Modeling and Applications*. Cambridge University Press.

Institute for Health Metrics and Evaluation. 2014. http://ihmeuw.org/2aw7. (accessed October 2014).

Lee, Jong-Wha, and Warwick J. McKibbin. 2003. "Globalization and Disease: The Case of SARS." Working Paper 2003/16, Australian National University, Canberra.

Lofgren, Hans. 2013. "Creating and Using Fiscal Space for Accelerated Development in Liberia." Policy Research Working Paper 6678, World Bank, Washington, DC.

Lofgren, Hans, Martin Cicowiez, and Carolina Diaz-Bonilla. 2013. "MAMS—A Computable General Equilibrium Model for Developing Country Strategy Analysis." In *Handbook of Computable General Equilibrium Modeling SET*, Vols. 1A and 1B, edited by Peter B. Dixon and Dale W. Jorgenson, 159. North Holland: Elsevier B.V.

Martin, Will, and Devashish Mitra. 2001. "Productivity Growth and Convergence in Agriculture and Manufacturing." *Economic Development and Cultural Change* 49 (2): 403–22.

Meltzer, Martin I., Charisma Y. Atkins, Scott Santibanez, Barbara Knust, Brett W. Petersen, Elizabeth D. Ervin, Stuart T. Nichol, Inger K. Damon, and Michael L. Washington. 2014. "Estimating the Future Number of Cases in the Ebola Epidemic—Liberia and Sierra Leone, 2014–2015." MMWR Surveillance Summary 63, U.S. Centers for Disease Control and Prevention, Atlanta, GA.

van der Mensbrugghe, Dominique. 2011. *LINKAGE Technical Reference Document: Version 7.1*. Washington, DC: World Bank.

———. 2013. "Modeling the Global Economy—Forward Looking Scenarios for Agriculture." In *Handbook of Computable General Equilibrium Modeling*, edited by Peter B. Dixon and Dale W. Jorgenson, 933–94. North Holland: Elsevier B.V.

Wang, Haidong, Laura Dwyer-Lindgren, Katherine T. Lofgren, Julie Knoll Rajaratnam, Jacob R. Marcus, Alison Levin-Rector, Carly E. Levitz, Alan D. Lopez, and Christopher J. L. Murray. 2012. "Age-Specific and Sex-Specific Mortality in 187 Countries, 1970–2010: A Systematic Analysis of the Global Burden of Disease Study 2010." *The Lancet* 380 (9859): 2071–94.

WHO (World Health Organization). 2014a. *Ebola Response Roadmap Situation Report* WHO, November 12.

———. 2014b. *Ebola Response Roadmap*. WHO, August 28.

———. 2014c. *Ebola Situation in Senegal Remains Stable*. WHO, September 12.

———. 2014d. *Nigeria and Senegal: Stable—for the Moment*. WHO.

WHO Ebola Response Team. 2014. "Ebola Virus Disease in West Africa—The First 9 Months of the Epidemic and Forward Projections." *New England Journal of Medicine* 371:1481–95.

WFP (World Food Program). 2011. "The State of Food Security and Nutrition in Sierra Leone."